The CURSE OF LONO

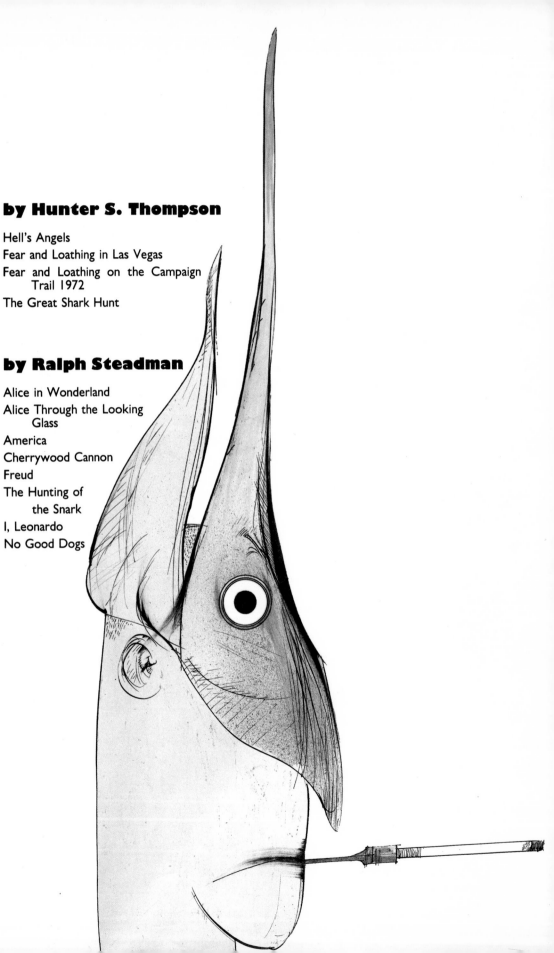

by Hunter S. Thompson

by Ralph Steadman

The CURSE OF LONO

by

Hunter S. Thompson

and

Ralph STEADman

Bantam Books

Toronto   ·   New York   ·   London   ·   Sydney

The CURSE OF LONO

A Bantam Book / November 1983

Grateful acknowledgment is made to the following for permission to quote
from copyrighted material:

From *The Last Voyage of Captain James Cook* by Richard Hough, copyright © 1979 by
Richard Hough. Used by permission of William Morrow & Co., Inc., and
Macmillan London Limited.

From *Hawaiian Monarchy: The Romantic Years* by Maxine Mrantz,
"The Law of the Splintered Oar" copyright © 1974 by Maxine Mrantz.
Used by permission of Aloha Graphics & Sales, Inc.

From "Hula Hula Boys" by Warren Zevon. Lyrics reprinted permission of
Zevon Music (BMI). Copyright © 1982 by Zevon Music.

Text copyright © 1983 by Hunter S. Thompson
Illustrations copyright © 1983 by Ralph Steadman

Produced by Laila Nabulsi.

Book design by Yaron Fidler.

Library of Congress Cataloging in Publication Data

Thompson, Hunter S.
The curse of Lono.

1. Thompson, Hunter S.   2. Journalists—United States—Biography.
3. Hawaii—Description and travel—1981-   I. Steadman, Ralph.   II. Title.
PN4874.T444A33   1983   070'.92'4 [B]   83-90660
ISBN 0-553-01387-4 (pbk.)

Published simultaneously in the United States and Canada

PRINTED IN THE UNITED STATES OF AMERICA

WAK   0   9   8   7

To my Mother, Virginia Ray Thompson

*Now it is not good for the Christian's health to hustle the
    Arian brown,*
*For the Christian riles, and the Arian smiles, and it weareth
    the Christian down;*
*And the end of the fight is a tombstone white with the name
    of the late deceased,*
*And the epitaph drear: 'A Fool lies here who tried to hustle
    the East.'*

Rudyard Kipling
"The Naulahka"

The Romantic God Lono

I have been writing a good deal, of late, about the great god Lono and Captain Cook's personation of him. Now, while I am here in Lono's home, upon ground which his terrible feet have trodden in remote ages—unless these natives lie, and they would hardly do that I suppose—I might as well tell who he was.

The idol the natives worshipped for him was a slender unornamented staff twelve feet long. Unpoetical history says he was a favorite god on the island of Hawaii—a great king who had been deified for meritorious services—just our fashion of rewarding heroes, with the difference that we would have made him a postmaster instead of a god, no doubt. In an angry moment he slew his wife, a goddess named Kaikilani Alii. Remorse of conscience drove him mad, and tradition presents us the singular spectacle of a god traveling "on the shoulder"; for in his gnawing grief he wandered about from place to place, boxing and wrestling with all whom he met. Of course this pastime soon lost its novelty, inasmuch as it must necessarily have been the case that when so powerful a deity sent a frail human opponent "to grass," he never came back anymore. Therefore he instituted games called makahiki, and ordered that they should be held in his honor, and then sailed for foreign lands on a three-cornered raft, stating that he would return some day, and that was the last of Lono. He was never seen anymore; his raft got swamped perhaps. But the people always expected his return, and they were easily led to accept Captain Cook as the restored god.

Mark Twain

Letters from Hawaii

Running

May 23, 1980

Hunter S. Thompson
c/o General Delivery
Woody Creek, CO

Dear Hunter:
  To keep a potential screed down to a few lines, we would like you to cover the Honolulu Marathon. We will pay all expenses and an excellent fee. Please contact us.

  Think about it. This is a good chance for a vacation.

Sincerely,

Paul Perry
Executive Editor,
Running Magazine

Dear Ralph,

I think we have a live one this time, old sport. Some dingbat named Perry up in Oregon wants to give us a month in Hawaii for Christmas and all we have to do is cover the Honolulu Marathon for his magazine, a thing called <u>Running</u>. . . .

Yeah, I know what you're thinking, Ralph. You're pacing around over there in the war room at the Old Loose Court and thinking, "Why <u>me</u>? And why <u>now</u>? Just when I'm getting respectable?"

Well . . . let's face it, Ralph; anybody can be respectable, especially in England. But not everybody can get paid to run like a bastard for 26 miles in some maniac hype race called the Honolulu Marathon.

We are both entered in this event, Ralph, and I feel pretty confident about winning. We will need a bit of training, but not much.

The main thing will be to run as an entry and set a killer pace for the first three miles. These body-nazis have been training all year for the supreme effort in this Super Bowl of marathons. The promoters expect 10,000 entrants, and the course is 26 miles; which means they will all start slow . . . because 26 miles is a hell of a long way to run, for any reason at all, and all the pros in this field will start slow and pace themselves very carefully for the first 20 miles.

But not us, Ralph. We will come out of the blocks like human torpedoes and alter the whole nature of the race by sprinting the first three miles shoulder-to-shoulder in under 10 minutes.

A pace like that will crack their nuts, Ralph. These people are into running, not <u>racing</u>—so our strategy will be to race like whorehounds <u>for the first three miles</u>. I figure we can crank ourselves up to a level of frenzy that will clock about 9:55 at the three-mile checkpoint . . . which will put us so far ahead of the field that they won't even be able to see us. We will be over the hill and all alone when we hit the stretch along Ala Moana Boulevard still running shoulder-to-shoulder at a pace so fast and crazy that not even the judges will feel sane about it . . . and the rest of the field will be left so far behind that many will be overcome with blind rage and confusion.

I've also entered you in the Pipeline Masters, a world class surfing contest on the north shore of Oahu on Dec. 26.

You will need some work on your high-speed balance for this one, Ralph. You'll be shot through the curl at speeds up to 50 or even 75 miles an hour, and you won't want to fall.

I won't be with you in the Pipeline gig, due to serious objections raised by my attorney with regard to the urine test and other legal ramifications.

But I will enter the infamous Liston Memorial Rooster Fight, at $1,000 per unit on the universal scale—e.g., one minute in the cage with one rooster wins $1,000 . . . or five minutes with one rooster is worth $5,000 . . . and two minutes with five roosters is $10,000 . . . etc.

This is serious business, Ralph. These Hawaiian slashing roosters can tear a man to shreds in a matter of seconds. I am training here at home with the peacocks—six 40-pound birds in a 6' × 6' cage, and I think I'm getting the hang of it.

The time has come to kick ass, Ralph, even if it means coming briefly out of retirement and dealing, once again, with the public. I am also in need of a rest—for legal reasons—so I want this gig to be _easy_, and I know in my heart that it will be.

Don't worry, Ralph. We will bend a few brains with this one. I have already secured the Compound: two homes with a 50-meter pool on the edge of the sea on Alii Drive in Kona, where the sun always shines.

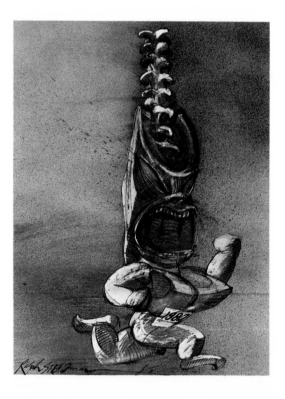

OK
HST

A 'doctored' Hunter S. Thompson drawing by →

THE BLUE ARM

We were about forty minutes out of San Francisco when the crew finally decided to take action on the problem in Lavatory 1B. The door had been locked since takeoff and now the chief stewardess had summoned the copilot down from the flight deck. He appeared in the aisle right beside me, carrying a strange-looking black tool in his hand, like a flashlight with blades, or some kind of electric chisel. He nodded calmly as he listened to the stewardess's urgent whispering. "I can talk to him," she said, pointing a long red fingernail at the "occupied" sign on the locked toilet door, "but I can't get him out."

The copilot nodded thoughtfully, keeping his back to the passengers while he made some adjustments on the commando tool he was holding. "Any ID?" he asked her.

She glanced at a list on her clipboard. "Mr. Ackerman," she said. "Address: Box 99, Kailua-Kona."

"The big island," he said.

She nodded, still consulting her clipboard. "Red Carpet Club member," she said. "Frequent traveler, no previous history . . . boarded in San Francisco, one-way first class to Honolulu. A perfect gentleman. No connections booked." She continued, "No hotel reservations, no rental cars . . ." She shrugged. "Very polite, sober, relaxed . . ."

"Yeah," he said. "I know the type." The officer stared down at his tool for a moment, then raised his other hand and knocked sharply on the door. "Mr. Ackerman?" he called. "Can you hear me?"

There was no answer, but I was close enough to the door to hear sounds of movement inside: first, the bang of a toilet seat dropping, then running water. . . .

I didn't know Mr. Ackerman, but I remembered him coming aboard. He had the look of a man who had once been a tennis pro in Hong Kong, then gone on to bigger things. The gold Rolex, the white linen bush jacket, the Thai Bhat chain around his neck, the heavy leather briefcase with combination locks on every zipper. . . . These were not signs of a man who would lock himself in the bathroom immediately after takeoff and stay inside for almost an hour.

Which is too long, on any flight. That kind of behavior raises questions that eventually become hard to ignore—especially in the spacious first-class compartment on a 747 on a five-hour flight to Hawaii. People who pay that kind of money don't like the idea of having to stand in line to use the only available bathroom, while something clearly wrong is going on in the other one.

I was one of these people. . . . My social contract with United Airlines entitled me, I felt, to at least the use of a tin stand-up bathroom with a lock on the door for as long as I needed to get myself cleaned up. I had spent six hours hanging around the Red Carpet Room in the San Francisco airport, arguing with ticket agents, drinking heavily and fending off waves of strange memories. . . .

About halfway between Denver and San Francisco, we'd decided to change planes and get on a 747 for the next leg. The DC-10 is nice for short hops and sleeping, but the 747 is far better for the working professional on a long haul—because the 747 has a dome lounge, a sort of club car on top of the plane with couches and wooden card tables and its own separate bar, which can only be reached by an iron spiral staircase in the first-class compartment. It meant taking the chance of losing the luggage, and a tortured layover in the San Francisco airport . . . but I needed room to work, to spread out a bit, and maybe even sprawl.

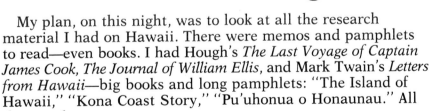

My plan, on this night, was to look at all the research material I had on Hawaii. There were memos and pamphlets to read—even books. I had Hough's *The Last Voyage of Captain James Cook*, *The Journal of William Ellis*, and Mark Twain's *Letters from Hawaii*—big books and long pamphlets: "The Island of Hawaii," "Kona Coast Story," "Pu'uhonua o Honaunau." All these and many more.

"You can't just come out here and write about the marathon," my friend John Wilbur had told me. "There's a hell of a lot more to Hawaii than ten thousand Japs running past Pearl Harbor. Come on out," he said. "These islands are full of mystery, never mind Don Ho and all the tourist gibberish—there's a hell of a lot more here than most people understand."

Wonderful, I thought—Wilbur is wise. Anybody who can move from the Washington Redskins to a house on the beach in Honolulu must understand something about life that I don't.

Indeed. Deal with the mystery. Do it now. Anything that can create itself by erupting out of the bowels of the Pacific Ocean is worth looking at.

After six hours of failure and drunken confusion, I had finally secured two seats on the last 747 flight of the day to Honolulu.

Now I needed a place to shave, brush my teeth, and maybe just stand there and look at myself in the mirror and wonder, as always, who might be looking back.

There is no possible economic argument for a genuinely private place of *any* kind on a ten million dollar flying machine. The risk is too high.

No. That makes no sense. Too many people like Master Sergeants forced into early retirement have tried to set themselves on fire in these tin cubicles . . . too many psychotics and half-mad dope addicts have locked themselves inside, then gobbled pills and tried to flush themselves down the long blue tube.

The copilot rapped on the door with his knuckles. "Mr. Ackerman! Are you all right?"

He hesitated, then called again, much louder this time. "Mr. Ackerman! This is your captain speaking. Are you sick?"

"What?" said a voice from inside.

The stewardess leaned close to the door. "This is a medical emergency, Mr. Ackerman—we can get you out of there in thirty seconds if we have to." She smiled triumphantly at Captain Goodwrench as the voice inside came alive again.

"I'm fine," it said. "I'll be out in a minute."

The copilot stood back and watched the door. There were more sounds of movement inside—but nothing else, except the sound of running water.

By this time the entire first class cabin was alerted to the crisis. "Get that freak out of there!" an old man shouted. "He might have a bomb!"

"Oh my God!" a woman screamed. "He's in there with something!"

The copilot flinched, then turned to face the passengers. He pointed his tool at the old man, who was now becoming hysterical. "You!" he snapped. "Shut up! I'll handle this."

Suddenly the door opened and Mr. Ackerman stepped out. He moved quickly into the aisle and smiled at the stewardess. "Sorry to keep you waiting," he said. "It's all yours now." He was backing down the aisle, his bush jacket draped casually over his arm, but not covering it.

From where I was sitting I could see that the arm he was trying to hide from the stewardess was bright blue, all the way up to the shoulder. The sight of it made me coil nervously into my seat. I had liked Mr. Ackerman, at first. He had the look of a man who might share my own tastes . . . but now he was looking like trouble, and I was ready to kick him in the balls like a mule for any reason at all. My original impression of the man had gone all to pieces by that time. This geek who had locked himself in the bathroom for so long that one of his arms had turned blue was not the same gracious, linen-draped Pacific yachtsman who had boarded the plane in San Francisco.

Most of the other passengers seemed happy enough just to see the problem come out of the bathroom peacefully: no sign of a weapon, no dynamite taped to his chest, no screaming of incomprehensible terrorist slogans or threatening to slit people's throats. . . . The old man was still sobbing quietly, not looking at Ackerman as he continued to back down the aisle toward his own seat, but nobody else seemed worried.

The copilot, however, was staring at Ackerman with an expression of pure horror on his face. He had seen the blue arm—and so had the stewardess, who was saying nothing at all. Ackerman was still trying to keep his arm hidden under the bush jacket. None of the other passengers had noticed it—or, if they had, they didn't know what it meant.

But I did, and so did the bug-eyed stewardess. The copilot gave Ackerman one last withering glance, then shuddered with obvious disgust as he closed up his commando tool and moved away. On his way to the spiral staircase that led back upstairs to the flight deck, he paused right above me in the aisle and whispered to Ackerman: "You filthy bastard, don't ever let me catch you on one of my flights again."

I saw Ackerman nod politely, then he slid into his seat just across the aisle from me. I quickly stood up and moved toward the bathroom with my shaving kit in my hand—and when I'd locked myself safely inside I carefully closed the toilet seat before I did anything else.

There is only one way to get your arm dyed blue on a 747 flying at 38,000 feet over the Pacific. But the truth is so rare and unlikely that not even the most frequent air travelers have ever had to confront it—and it is usually not a thing that the few who understand want to talk about.

The powerful disinfectant that most airlines use in their toilet-flushing facilities is a chemical compound known as Dejerm, which is colored a very vivid blue. The only other time I ever saw a man come out of an airplane bathroom with a blue arm was on a long flight from London to Zaire, en route to the Ali–Foreman fight. A British news correspondent from Reuters had gone into the bathroom and somehow managed to drop his only key to the Reuters telex machine in Kinshasa down the aluminum bowl. He emerged about 30 minutes later, and he had a whole row to himself the rest of the way to Zaire.

It was almost midnight when I emerged from Lavatory 1B and went back to my seat to gather up my research material. The overhead lights were out and the other passengers were sleeping. It was time to go upstairs to the dome lounge and get some work done. The Honolulu Marathon would be only one part of the story. The rest would have to deal with Hawaii itself, and that was something I'd never had any reason to even think about. I had a quart of Wild Turkey in my satchel, and I knew there was plenty of ice upstairs in the dome bar, which is usually empty at night.

But not this time. When I got to the top of the spiral staircase I saw my fellow traveler, Mr. Ackerman, sleeping peacefully on one of the couches near the bar. He woke up as I passed by on my way to a table in the rear, and I thought I saw a flicker of recognition in the weary smile on his face.

I nodded casually as I passed. "I hope you found it," I said.
He looked up at me. "Yeah," he said. "Of course."
By this time I was ten feet behind him and spreading my research materials out on the big card table. Whatever it was, I didn't want to know about it. He had his problems and I had mine. I had hoped to have the dome to myself for these hours, to be alone, but Mr. Ackerman was obviously settled in for the night. It was the only place on the plane where his presence wouldn't cause trouble. He would be with me for a while, so I figured we might as well get along.

There was a strong odor of disinfectant in the air. The whole dome smelled like the basement of a bad hospital. I opened all the air vents above my seat, then spread my research out on the table. I tried to remember if the British correspondent had suffered any pain or injury from his experience, but all that came to mind was that he wore heavy long-sleeved shirts the whole time he was in Zaire. No loss of flesh, no poison oil in the nervous system, but three weeks in the heat of the Congo had caused an awful fungus to come alive on his arm, and when I saw him in London two months later his hand was still noticeably blue.

I walked up to the bar and got some ice for my drink. On the way back to my desk I asked him, "How's your arm?"
"Blue," he replied. "And it itches."
I nodded. "That's powerful stuff. You should probably check with a doctor when you get to Honolulu."
He eased up in his seat and looked back at me. "Aren't *you* a doctor?" he asked.
"What?"
He smiled and lit a cigarette. "It's on your luggage tags," he said. "It says you're a doctor."
I laughed, and looked down at my satchel. Sure enough, the Red Carpet Club baggage tag said, "Dr. H. S. Thompson."

"Jesus," I said. "You're right. I *am* a doctor."

He shrugged.

"Okay," I said finally, "let's get that weird shit off your arm." I stood up and motioned him to follow me into the tiny "crew only" bathroom behind the flight deck. We spent the next 20 minutes scrubbing his arm with soap-soaked paper towels, then I rubbed it down with a jar of cold cream from my shaving kit.

A nasty red rash like poison ivy had broken out all over his arm, thousands of filthy little bubbles. . . . I went back to my bag for a tube of Desenex, to kill the itching. There was no way to get rid of the blue dye.

"What?" he said. "It won't wash off?"

"No," I told him. "Maybe two weeks in saltwater can dull it out. Get out in the surf, hang around on the beach."

He looked confused. "The beach?"

"Yeah," I said. "Just go out there and do it. Tell them whatever you have to, call it a birthmark. . . ."

He nodded. "Yeah. That's good, Doc—*what* blue arm? Right?"

"Right," I said. "Never apologize, never explain. Just act normal and bleach the bugger out. You'll be famous on Waikiki Beach."

He laughed. "Thanks, Doc. Maybe I can do you a favor sometime—what brings you to Hawaii?"

"Business," I said. "I'm covering the Honolulu Marathon for a medical journal."

He nodded and sat down, stretching his blue arm out on the couch to give it some air. "Well," he said finally, "whatever you say, Doc." He grinned mischievously. *"A medical journal.* Jesus, that's good."

"What?"

He nodded thoughtfully and put his feet up on the table in front of him, then turned to smile at me. "I was just wondering how I might return the favor," he said. "You staying long in the islands?"

"Not in Honolulu," I said. "Just until after the Marathon on Saturday, then we're going over to a place called Kona."

"Kona?"

"Yeah," I said, leaning back and opening one of my books, a nineteenth-century volume titled *The Journal of William Ellis.*

He leaned back on the cushions and closed his eyes again. "It's a nice place," he said. "You'll like it."

"Well," I said, "that's good to know. I've already paid for it."

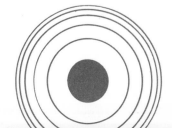

"Paid?"

"Yeah. I rented two houses on the beach."

He looked up. "You paid *in advance*?"

I nodded. "That was the only way I could get anything," I said. "The whole place is booked up."

"What?" He jerked up in his seat and stared back at me. "Booked up? What the hell are you renting—the Kona Village?"

I shook my head. "No," I said. "It's some kind of estate with two big houses and a pool, pretty far out of town."

"Where?" he asked.

There was something wrong with the tone of his voice, but I tried to ignore it. Whatever he was about to tell me, I felt, was something I didn't want to hear. "Some friends found it for me," I said quickly. "It's right on the beach. Totally private. We have to get a lot of work done."

Now he was definitely looking troubled. "Who'd you rent it from?" he asked. And then he mentioned the name of the real estate agent that I had, in fact, rented it from. The look on my face must have alarmed him, because he instantly changed the subject.

"Why Kona?" he asked. "You want to catch fish?"

I shrugged. "Not especially. But I want to get out on the water, do some diving. A friend of mine has a boat over there."

"Oh? Who's that?"

"A guy from Honolulu," I said. "Gene Skinner."

He nodded. "Yeah," he said. "Sure, I know Gene—The Blue Boar." He leaned up from the cushions and turned to look back at me, no longer half asleep. "He's a friend of yours?"

I nodded, surprised by the smile on his face. It was a smile I had seen before, but for a moment I couldn't place it.

Ackerman was still looking at me, an odd new light in his eyes. "Haven't seen him in a while," he said. "He's back in Hawaii?"

Whoops, I thought. Something wrong here. I recognized that smile now; I had seen it on the faces of other men, in other countries, at the mention of Skinner's name.

"Who?" I said, standing up to get some more ice.

"Skinner," he said.

"Back from where?" I wanted no part of Skinner's ancient feuds.

He seemed to understand. "You know anybody else in Kona?" he asked. "Besides Skinner?"

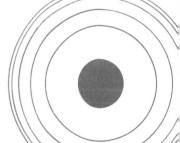

"Yeah," I said. "I know some people in the whiskey business. I know some real estate agents."

He nodded thoughtfully, staring down at the long fingers of his freshly-blued hand as if he'd just noticed something odd about it. I recognized the professional pause of a man long accustomed to the sound of his own brain working. I could

almost hear it—the high-speed memory-scan of a very personal computer that would sooner or later come up with whatever fact, link, or long-forgotten detail he was waiting for.

He closed his eyes again. "The big island is different from the others," he said. "Especially that mess in Honolulu. It's like going back in time. Nobody hassles you, plenty of space to move around. It's probably the only place in the islands where the people have any sense of the old Hawaiian culture."

"Wonderful," I said. "We'll be there next week. All we have to do in Honolulu is cover the Marathon, then hide out in Kona for a while and lash the story together."

"Right," he said. "Call me when you get settled in. I can take you around to some of the places where the old magic still lives." He smiled thoughtfully. "Yeah, we can go down to South Point, the City of Refuge, spend some time with the ghost of Captain Cook. Hell, we might even do some diving— if the weather's right."

I put my book down and we talked for a while. It was the first time anybody had ever told me anything interesting about Hawaii— the native legends, old wars, missionaries, the strange and terrible fate of Captain Cook.

"This City of Refuge looks interesting," I said. "You don't find many cultures with a sense of sanctuary that powerful."

"Yeah," he said, "but you had to *get there* first, and you had to be faster than whoever was chasing you."

City of Refuge at Honaunau

Adjoining the Hare o Keave to the southward, we found a Pahu tabu (sacred enclosure) of considerable extent, and were informed by our guide that it was one of the puhonuas of Hawaii, of which we had so often heard the chiefs and others speak. There are only two on the island; the one which we were then examining, and another at Waipio, on the north-east part of the island, in the district of Kohala.

These puhonuas were the Hawaiian cities of refuge, and afforded an inviolable sanctuary to the guilty fugitive who, when flying from the avenging spear, was so favoured as to enter their precincts.

This had several wide entrances, some on the side next the sea, the others facing the mountains. Hither the manslayer, the man who had broken a tabu, or failed in the observance of its rigid requirements, the thief, and even the murderer, fled from his incensed pursuers, and was secure.

To whomsoever he belonged, and from whatever part he came, he was equally certain of admittance, though liable to be pursued even to the gates of the enclosure.

Happily for him, those gates were perpetually open; and as soon as the fugitive had entered, he repaired to the presence of the idol, and made a short ejaculatory address, expressive of his obligations to him in reaching the place with security.

The priests, and their adherents, would immediately put to death any one who should have the temerity to follow or molest those who were once within the pale of the pahu tabu; and, as they expressed it, under the shade or protection of the spirit of Keave, the tutelar deity of the place.

We could not learn the length of time it was necessary for them to remain in the puhonua; but it did not appear to be more than two or three days. After that, they either attached themselves to the service of the priests, or returned to their homes.

The puhonua at Honaunau is capacious, capable of containing a vast multitude of people. In time of war, the females, children, and old people of the neighboring districts, were generally left within it, while the men went to battle. Here they awaited in safety the issue of the conflict, and were secure against surprise and destruction, in the event of a defeat.

The Journal of William Ellis

(Circa 1850)

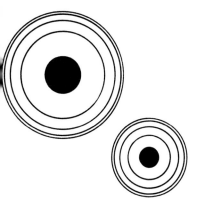
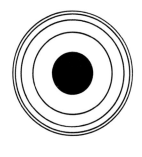
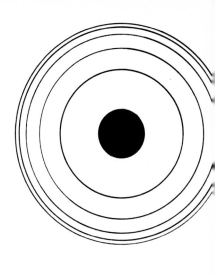

He chuckled. "It was a sporting proposition, for sure."

"But once you got there," I said, "you were absolutely protected—right?"

"Absolutely," he said. "Not even the gods could touch you, once you got through the gate."

"Wonderful," I said. "I might need a place like that."

"Yeah," he said. "Me too. That's why I live where I do."

"Where?"

He smiled. "On a clear day I can look down the mountain and see the City of Refuge from my front porch. It gives me a great sense of comfort."

I had a feeling that he was telling the truth. Whatever kind of life Ackerman lived seemed to require a built-in fall-back position. You don't find many investment counselors from Hawaii or anywhere else who can drop anything so important down the tube in a 747 bathroom that they will get their arms dyed bright blue to retrieve it.

We were alone in the dome, 38,000 feet above the Pacific with at least another two hours to go. We would be in Honolulu sometime around sunrise. Over the top of my book I could see him half-asleep but constantly scratching his arm. His eyes were closed, but the fingers of his clean hand were wide awake and his spastic movements were beginning to get on my nerves.

The stewardess came up to have a look at us, but the sight of Ackerman's arm made her face quiver and she quickly went back down the stairs. We had a small icebox full of Miller High Life and a whole selection of mini-bottles in the liquor drawer, so there was no need to do anything but keep a wary eye on Ackerman.

Finally he seemed to be asleep. The dome was dark, except for the small glow of table lights, and I settled back on the couch to ponder my research material.

The main impression I recall from what I read in those hours is that the Hawaiian Islands had no written history at all beyond the past two hundred years, when the first missionaries and sea captains began trying to interpret a chronology of some kind by listening to tales told by natives. Nobody even knew where the islands themselves had come from, much less the people.

On the gray afternoon of January 16, 1779, Captain James Cook, the greatest explorer of his age, sailed the two ships of his Third Pacific Expedition into the tiny rock-walled shelter of Kealakekua Bay on the west coast of a previously uncharted mid-Pacific island called "Owhyhee" by the natives, and found his place in history as the first white man to officially "discover" the Hawaiian Islands.

The bay inside the channel was shrouded in fog and surrounded by a wall of sheer cliffs, 500 feet high. It looked more like a tomb than a harbor, and—despite the desperate condition of his ships and his crews after ten days in a killer monsoon—Cook was reluctant to enter. But he had no choice: his crew was threatening mutiny, scurvy was rampant, his ships were coming apart beneath his feet, and the morale of his whole Expedition had collapsed after six months at sea in the Arctic. . . . And now, after sailing straight south from Alaska in a condition of genuine hysteria, the mere sight of land made them crazy.

So Cook took them in. Kealakekua Bay wasn't the kind of safe anchorage he wanted. But it was the only one available in what turned out to be his last storm.

Early on the morning of 16 January [1779], Cook said to his master, "Mr. Bligh, be so good as to take a boat, well armed, and take soundings." They could both make out what Cook called "the appearance of a bay."

"It seems promising, sir, and the indians friendly enough," said Bligh.

Cook spoke harshly. "Whatever the nature of the indians, if it is a safe anchorage, I shall resolve to anchor in it. This has been a poor island for shelter and our need to refit is very great."

Bligh, accompanied by Edgar in a boat from the *Discovery*, set his men to row on a north-easterly heading for a deep cup cut into the cliffs, meeting on the way a great armada of canoes of many sizes, all bustling towards the ships at twice their own speed and waving their paddles and streamers and singing out as they passed.

As Bligh closed the shore he became more than ever confident that this would be a safe anchorage for them. It appeared protected from all points, except the south-west, and from his recent observations gales from this quarter were unlikely. The dominant feature of this bay was a cliff like a knife-cut through black volcanic rock in a slight curve, falling from some 400 feet at the eastern extremity to a point a mile to the west where it shelved into gently rising land from the western promontory of the bay. This cliff, this black insurmountable barrier to the hinterland, appeared to fall directly to the sea, but as the day wore on and the tide ebbed, Bligh observed that there was a narrow beach at its base—black rocks and pebbles. As they were to learn later, the name of this bay, Kealakekua (Karakakooa, Cook called it) means "path of the gods," deriving from this great slide in the hill to the sea.

Richard Hough

The Last Voyage of Captain James Cook

I was still reading when the stewardess appeared to announce that we'd be landing in thirty minutes. "You'll have to take your regular seats down below," she said, not looking at Ackerman, who still seemed asleep.

I began packing up my gear. The sky outside the portholes was getting light. As I dragged my satchel up the aisle Ackerman woke up and lit a cigarette. "Tell 'em I couldn't make it," he said. "I think I can handle the landing from up here." He grinned and fastened a seat belt that poked out from the depths of the couch. "They won't miss me down there," he said. "I'll see you in Kona."

"Okay," I said. "You're not staying in Honolulu?"

He shook his head. "Just long enough to get to the bank," he said, glancing down at his watch. "It opens at nine. I should be home for lunch."

I stopped and shook hands with him. "Good luck," I said. "Take care of that arm."

He smiled and reached into the pocket of his bush jacket. "Thanks, Doc," he said. "Here's a little something for you. It might be a long day." He dropped a small glass bottle in my hand and pointed to the crew bathroom. "Better do it up here," he said. "You don't want to be landing with anything illegal."

I agreed and went quickly into the tin closet. When I came out I tossed the bottle back to him. "Wonderful," I said. "I feel better already."

"That's good," he replied. "I have the feeling you're going to need all the help you can get over here."

ADVENTURES IN THE DUMB LIFE

My friend Gene Skinner met us at the airport in Honolulu, parking his black GTO convertible up on the sidewalk by the baggage carousel and fending off public complaints with a distracted wave of his hand and the speedy behavior of a man with serious business on his mind. He was pacing back and forth in front of his car, sipping from a brown bottle of Primo beer and ignoring the oriental woman wearing a meter maid's uniform who was trying to get his attention as he scanned the baggage lobby.

I saw him from the top of the escalator and I knew we would have to be quick with the luggage transfer. Skinner was so accustomed to working in war zones that he would not see anything wrong with driving up on the sidewalk in the middle of an angry crowd to pick up whatever he'd come for . . . which was *me*, in this case, so I hurried toward him with a businesslike smile on my face. "Don't worry," he was saying. "We'll be out of here in a minute."

Most people seemed to believe him, or at least wanted to. Everything about him suggested a person who was better left alone. The black GTO had a menacing appearance, and Skinner looked meaner than the car. He was wearing a white linen reef jacket with at least thirteen custom-built pockets to fit everything from a phosphorous grenade to a waterproof pen. His blue silk slacks were sharply creased and he wore no socks, only cheap rubber sandals that slapped on the tile as he paced. He was a head taller than anyone else in the airport and his eyes were hidden behind blue-black Saigon-mirror sunglasses. The heavy, square-linked gold Bhat chain around his neck could only have been bought in some midnight jewelry store on a back street in Bangkok, and the watch on his wrist was a gold Rolex with a stainless steel band. His whole presence was out of place in a crowd of mainland tourists shuffling off an Aloha flight from San Francisco. Skinner was not on vacation.

He saw me as I approached, and held out his hand. "Hello, Doc," he said with a curious smile. "I thought you quit this business."

"I did," I said. "But I got bored."

"Me too," he said. "I was on my way out of town when they called me. Somebody from the Marathon committee. They needed an official photographer, for a thousand dollars a day."

He glanced down at a brace of new-looking Nikons on the front seat of the GTO. "I couldn't turn them down," he said. "It's free money."

"Jesus," I said, "you're a photographer now?"

He stared down at his feet for a moment, then pivoted slowly to face me, rolling his eyes and baring his teeth to the sun. "This is the Eighties, Doc. I'm whatever I need to be."

Skinner was no stranger to money. Or to lying, either, for that matter. When I knew him in Saigon he was working for the CIA, flying helicopters for Air America and making what some people who knew him said was more than $20,000 a week in the opium business.

I never talked about money with him and he had a visceral hatred of journalists, but we soon became friends and I spent a lot of time during the last weeks of the war smoking opium with him on the floor of his room in the Continental Palace. Mr. Hee brought the pipe every afternoon around three—even on the day his house in Cholon was hit by a rocket—and the guests lay down in silence to receive the magic smoke.

That is still one of my clearest memories of Saigon—stretching out on the floor with my cheek on the cool white tile and the dreamy soprano babble of Mr. Hee in my ears as he slithered around the room with his long black pipe and his little bunsen burner, constantly refilling the bowl and chanting intensely in a language that none of us knew.

"Who are you working for these days?" Skinner asked.

"I'm covering the race for a medical journal," I said.

"Wonderful," he said quickly. "We can use a good medical connection. What kind of drugs are you carrying?"

"Nothing," I said. "Absolutely nothing."

He shrugged, then looked up as the carousel began moving and the bags started coming down the chute. "Whatever you say, Doc," he said. "Let's load your stuff in the car and get out of here before they grab me for felony menacing. I'm not in the mood to argue with these people."

The crowd was getting restive and the oriental policewoman was writing a ticket. I lifted the beer bottle out of his hand and took a long swallow, then tossed my leather satchel in the back seat of his car and introduced him to my fiancée. "You must be crazy," she said, "to park on a sidewalk like this."

"That's what I get paid for," he said. "If I was sane we'd have to carry your bags all the way to the parking lot."

She eyed him warily as we began loading luggage. "Stand aside!" he barked at a child who had wandered in front of the car. "Do you want to be killed?"

The crowd fell back at that point. Whatever we were doing

was not worth getting killed for. The child disappeared as I trundled a big aluminum suitcase off the carousel, almost dropping it as I tossed it back to Skinner, who caught it before it could bounce and tucked it neatly into the back seat of the convertible.

The meter maid was writing another citation, our third in ten minutes, and I could see she was losing her grip. "I give you sixty seconds," she screamed. "Then I have you towed away!"

He patted her affectionately on the shoulder, then got in the car and started the engine, which came suddenly alive with a harsh metallic roar. "You're too pretty for this kind of chickenshit work," he said, handing her a card that he'd picked off his dashboard. "Call me at the office," he told her. "You should be posing for naked postcards."

"What?" she yelled, as he eased the car into reverse.

The crowd parted sullenly, not happy to see us escape. "Call the police!" somebody shouted. The meter maid was yelling into her walkie-talkie as we moved into traffic, leaving our engine noise behind.

Skinner lifted another bottle of Primo out of a small plastic cooler on the floor of the front seat, then steered with his knees while he jerked off the top and lit a cigarette. "Where to, Doc?" he asked. "The Kahala Hilton?"

"Right," I said. "How far is it?"

"Far," he said. "We'll have to stop for more beer."

I leaned back on the hot leather seat and closed my eyes. There was a strange song about "hula hula boys" on the radio, a Warren Zevon tune:

> . . . Ha'ina 'ia mai ana ka puana
> Ha'ina 'ia mai ana ka puana . . .
>
> I saw her leave the luau
> With the one who parked the cars
> And the fat one from the swimming pool
> They were swaying arm in arm . . .

Skinner stomped on the gas and we shot through a sudden opening to the inside, missing the tailgate of a slow-moving pineapple truck by six inches and swooping through a pack of mongrel dogs on their way across the highway. We hit gravel and the rear end started coming around, but Skinner straightened it out. The dogs held their ground for an instant, then scattered in panic as he leaned out of the car and smacked one of them on the side of the head with his beer bottle. He was a big yellow brute with scrawny flanks and the long dumb jaw of a tenth-generation cur; and he had charged the GTO with the back-alley dumbness of a bully that had been charging things all his life, and always seen them back off. He came straight at the left front wheel, yapping wildly, and his eyes got suddenly huge when he realized, too late, that Skinner was not going to swerve. He braced all four paws on the hot asphalt, but he was charging too fast to stop. The GTO was going about fifty in low gear. Skinner kept his foot on the accelerator and swung the bottle like a polo mallet. I heard a muffled smack, then a hideous yelping screech as the beast went tumbling across the highway and under the wheels of the pineapple truck, which crushed it.

"They're a menace," he said, tossing the neck of the bottle away. "Utterly vicious. They'll jump right into your car at a stoplight. It's one of the problems with driving a convertible."

My fiancée was weeping hysterically and the warped tune was still coming out of the radio:

> *I could hear their ukeleles playing*
> *Down by the sea . . .*
> *She's gone with the hula hula boys*
> *She don't care about me*
>
> *Ha'ina 'ia mai ana ka puana*
> *Ha'ina 'ia mai ana ka puana . . .*

Skinner slowed down as we approached the exit to downtown Honolulu. "Okay, Doc," he said. "It's time to break out the drugs. I feel nervous."

Indeed, I thought. You murdering swine. "Ralph has it," I said quickly. "He's waiting for us at the hotel. He has a whole Alka-Seltzer bottle full of it."

He moved his foot off the brake and back to the accelerator as we passed under a big green sign that said "Waikiki Beach 1½." The smile on his face was familiar. The giddy, screw-headed smirk of a dope fiend ready to pounce. I knew it well.

"Ralph is paranoid," I said. "We'll have to be careful with him."

"Don't worry about me," he said. "I get along fine with the English."

We were in downtown Honolulu now, cruising along the waterfront. The streets were full of joggers fine-tuning their strides for the big race. They ignored passing traffic, which made Skinner nervous.

"This running thing is out of control," he said. "Every rich liberal in the Western world is into it. They run ten miles a day. It's a goddamn religion."

"Do *you* run?" I asked.

He laughed. "Hell yes, I run. But never with empty hands. We're *criminals*, Doc. We're not *like* these people and I think we're too old to learn."

"But we *are* professionals," I said. "And we're here to cover the race."

"Fuck the race," he said. "We'll cover it from Wilbur's front yard—get drunk and gamble heavily on the football games."

John Wilbur, a pulling guard on the Washington Redskins team that went to the Super Bowl in 1973, was another old friend from the white-knuckle days of yesteryear, who had finally settled down enough to pass for a respectable businessman in Honolulu. His house on Kahala Drive in the high-rent section was situated right on the course for this race, about two miles from the finish line. . . . It would be a perfect headquarters for our coverage, Skinner explained. We would catch the start downtown, then rush out to Wilbur's to watch the games and abuse the runners as they came by the house, then rush back downtown in time to cover the finish.

"Good planning," I said. "This looks like my kind of story."

"Not really," he said. "You've never seen anything as dull as one of these silly marathons . . . but it's a good excuse to get crazy."

"That's what I mean," I said. "I'm *entered* in this goddamn race." He shook his head. "Forget it," he said. "Wilbur tried to pull a Rosie Ruiz a few years ago, when he was still in top shape—he jumped into the race about a half mile ahead of everybody at the twenty-four-mile mark, and took off like a bastard for the finish line, running at what he figured was his normal 880 speed. . . ." He laughed. "It was horrible," he continued. "Nineteen people passed him in two miles. He went blind from vomiting and had to crawl the last hundred yards." He laughed again. "These people are *fast*, man. They ran right over him."

"Well," I said, "so much for that. I didn't want to enter this goddamn thing anyway. It was Wilbur's idea."

"That figures," he said. "You want to be careful out here. Even your best friends will lie to you. They can't help themselves."

We found Ralph slumped at the bar in the Ho-Ho Lounge, cursing the rain and the surf and the heat and everything else in Honolulu. He had waded out from the beach for a bit of the fine snorkeling that Wilbur had told us about—but before he could even get his head in the water a wave lifted him up and slammed him savagely into a coral head, ripping a hole in his back and crushing a disc in his spine. Skinner tried to cheer him up with a few local horror stories, but Ralph would have none of it. His mood was ugly, and it became even uglier when Skinner demanded cocaine.

"What are you *talking* about?" Ralph screamed. "The Dumb Dust, man," Skinner said. "The *lash*, the *crank*, the white death . . . I don't know what you limeys call it. . . ." "You mean *drugs*?" Ralph said finally. "OF COURSE I MEAN DRUGS!" Skinner screamed. "You think I came here to talk about *art*?" That finished that. Ralph limped away in a funk, and even the bartender got weird.

FIRE IN THE NUTS

We settled down at the bar and watched the rain lash the palm trees around on the beach. The Ho Ho Lounge was open on three sides and every few minutes a gust of warm rain blew in from the sea.

We were the only customers. The Samoan bartender mixed our margaritas in silence, a rigid smile on his face. To our left, on a rock in a small freshwater pool, two penguins stood solemnly side by side and watched us drinking, their deep unblinking brown eyes as curious as the bartender's.

Skinner tossed them a chunk of *sashimi*, which the taller one caught in mid-air and gobbled instantly, whacking the smaller bird out of his way with a flip of his short black wing.

"Those birds are weird," Skinner said. "I've had some real peculiar conversations with them."

He had sulked for a while after Ralph spiked his vision of wallowing in pure London Merck for the rest of the day, but he accepted it as just another one of those illogical flare-ups that come with the territory.

After three or four rounds the glint was back in his voice and he was looking at the penguins with the lazy eyes of a man who would not be bored too much longer.

"They're a husband and wife team," he said. "The old man is the big one; he'd peddle her ass for a handful of fish." He glanced over at me. "You think Ralph likes penguins?"

I stared at the bird.

"Never mind," he said. "He'd probably kill the poor beast anyway. The British will fuck anything. They're all perverts."

The bartender had his back to us, but I knew he was listening. The rigid smile on his face was looking more and more like a grimace. How many times had he stood calmly back there on the duckboards and listened to respectable-looking people talk about raping the hotel penguins?

"How long is this goddamn rain going to last?" I asked.

Skinner looked out at the beach. "God knows," he said. "This is what they call 'Kona Weather.' The winds get turned around

---

On the first day of December [1778] . . . he recognized that he was raising the greatest of all the islands he had discovered: what the natives appeared to call, and Cook wrote, "Owhyhee." By the next morning they were close in to the spectacular shore of massive cliffs, spines of land thrusting out into headlands, white streaks of great waterfalls tumbling into the white surf, more rivers emerging from deep valleys. Inland there were ravines with thundering torrents, a landscape of mixed barrenness and fruitfulness, a pocked landscape rising slowly and then higher and higher to the summits that were snow-capped. Snow in the tropics! Another new discovery, another new paradox. Here, it seemed, was another rich land, and far greater in extent than even Tahiti. Through a telescope, thousands of natives could be seen pouring from their dwellings and their places of work, and streaming towards the cliff tops to stare out and hold aloft white strips of cloth as if greeting a new messiah.

Richard Hough

The Last Voyage of Captain James Cook

---

and the weather comes up from the south. Sometimes it lasts for nine or ten days."

I didn't really care. It was enough, at this point, to be away from the snow drifts on my porch in Colorado. We called for another brace of margaritas and relaxed to talk for a while. I kept one eye on the bartender while Skinner told me about Hawaii.

People get edgy when the Kona weather hits. After nine or ten straight days of high surf and no sun you can get your spleen kicked completely out of your body on any street in Honolulu, just for honking at a Samoan. There is a large and increasingly obvious Samoan population in Hawaii. They are big, dangerous people with uncontrollable tempers and their hearts are filled with hate by the sound of an automobile horn, regardless of who's getting honked at.

Caucasians are called "haole people" by the native Hawaiians and racial violence is a standard item in the daily newspapers and on the evening TV news.

The stories are grisly, and a few are probably true. A current favorite in Waikiki is the one about "A whole family from San Francisco"—a lawyer, his wife and three children—who got raped by a gang of Koreans while strolling on the beach at sunset, so close to the Hilton that people sipping pineapple daiquiris on the hotel veranda heard their screams until long after dark, but they shrugged off the noise as nothing more than the shrieking of sea gulls in a feeding frenzy.

"Don't go *near* the beach after dark," Skinner warned, "unless you feel *seriously* bored."

The Korean community in Honolulu is not ready, yet, for the melting pot. They are feared by the *haoles*, despised by the Japs and Chinese, scorned by Hawaiians and occasionally hunted for sport by gangs of drunken Samoans, who consider them vermin, like wharf rats and stray dogs. . . .

"And stay *away* from Korean bars," Skinner added. "They're degenerate scum—cruel, bloodthirsty little bastards. They're meaner than rats and a hell of a lot bigger than most dogs, and they can kick the shit out of anything that walks on two legs, except maybe a Samoan."

I shot a quick look at our bartender, shifting my weight on the stool and planting both feet on the floor. But he was working the adding machine, apparently deaf to Skinner's raving. What the hell? I thought. He can only catch one of us. I picked my Zippo off the bar and casually buttoned my wallet-pocket.

"My grandfather was Korean," I said. "Where can we meet these people?"

"What?" he said. "*Meet* them?"

"Don't worry," I said. "They'll know me."

"Fuck 'em," he said. "They're not people. It'll be another hundred years before we can even think about letting Koreans mate with anything human."

I felt vaguely sick, but said nothing. The bartender was still engrossed in his money-work.

"Forget it," Skinner said. "Let me tell you a negro story. It'll get your mind off Koreans."

"I've heard it," I said. "The girl who got pushed off the cliff?"

"Right," he said. "It scared the shit out of *everybody*." He lowered his voice and leaned closer to me. "I knew her well," he said. "She was *beautiful*, a senior stewardess for Pan Am."

I nodded.

"For *no reason at all*," he went on. "She was just standing there on the edge, with her boyfriend—up there on that peak where they take all the tourists—when all of a sudden this crazy nigger just runs up behind her and gives a big shove. Whacko! Right off the edge and a thousand feet down to the beach." He nodded grimly. "She bounced two or three times off a waterfall about halfway down, then she went out of sight. They never saw her again, never found the first trace of her body."

"Why?" I wondered.

"Who knows?" he replied. "They never even put him on trial. He was declared 'hopelessly insane.' "

"Yeah," I said. "I remember it—*the black fiend who wore earphones*, right? The same guy who got busted a few weeks earlier for trying to run naked in the Marathon?"

"Yeah, the fastest crazy nigger in the world. He ran about half the race stark naked, before they finally caught him. The bastard was *fast*," he said, smiling slightly. "It took ten cops on motorcycles to run him down and put the net on him. He was some kind of world-class runner before he flipped out."

"Balls," I said. "That's no excuse. These brainless murdering freaks should be castrated."

"Absolutely," he said. "It's already happened."

"What?"

"The Samoans," he said. "The traffic jam on the freeway. . . . Jesus! You never heard *that* story?"

I shook my head.

"Okay," he said. "This is a wonderful story about how your worst nightmares can come true at any moment, with no warning at all."

"Good," I said. "Let's hear it. I like these stories. They speak to my deepest fears."

"They should," he said. "Paranoia pays, over here."

"What about the Samoans?"

"The Samoans?" He stared into his drink for a moment, then looked up. "All six of them went free. Nobody would testify.... Some poor bastard got caught in one of those Sunday afternoon traffic jams on the Pali Highway behind a pickup truck full of drunken Samoans. His car heated up like a bomb, but there was nothing he could do—no exit, no place he could even park it and flee. The Samoans did things like kick out his headlights and piss all over the hood of his car, but he hung on for almost two hours—with his doors locked and all his windows rolled up—until he finally passed out from heat exhaustion, and fell on his horn....

"The Samoans went instantly crazy," he continued. "They bashed out his windshield with tire irons, then they dragged him out and castrated him. Five of them held him down on the hood, while the other one sliced off his nuts—right in the middle of the Pali Highway on a Sunday afternoon."

I was watching the bartender very carefully now. The muscles on the back of his neck seemed to be bunching up, but I couldn't be sure. Skinner was still slumped on his stool, not ready to do anything fast. The stairs to the lobby were only about twenty feet away and I knew I could get there before the brute got his hands on me.

But he was still calm. Skinner ordered another round of margaritas and asked for the tab, which he paid with a gold American Express card.

Suddenly the phone behind the bar erupted with a burst of sharp rings. It was my fiancée, ringing down from the room.

Sportswriters were calling, she said. Word was out that Ralph and I were entered in the Marathon.

"Don't talk to the bastards," I warned her. "Anything you say will get us in trouble."

"I already talked to one of them," she said. "He knocked on the door and said he was Bob Arum."

"That's good," I said. "Bob's okay."

"It wasn't Arum," she said. "It was that geek we met in Vegas, the guy from the *New York Post*."

"Lock the door," I said. "It's Marley. Tell him I'm sick. They took me off the plane in Hilo. You don't know the name of the doctor."

"What about the race?" she asked. "What should I say?"

"It's out of the question," I said. "We're *both* sick. Tell them to leave us alone. We are victims of a publicity stunt."

"You fool," she snapped. "What did you *tell* these people?"

"Nothing," I said. "It was Wilbur. His mouth runs like jelly."

"He called," she said. "He'll be here at nine with a limo to pick us up for the party."

"What party?" I said, waving my hand to get Skinner's attention. "Is there a Marathon party tonight?" I asked him.

He pulled a piece of white paper from one of the pockets in his bush jacket. "Here's the schedule," he said. "Yeah, it's a private thing at Doc Scaff's house. Cocktails and dinner for the runners. We're invited."

I turned back to the phone. "What's the room number? I'll be up in a minute. There *is* a party. Hang on to the limo."

"You better talk to Ralph," she said. "He's very unhappy."

"So what?" I said. "He's an artist."

"You bastard!" she said. "You'd better be nice to Ralph. He came all the way from England—and he brought his wife and his daughter, just because you said so."

"Don't worry," I said. "He'll get what he came for."

"What?" she screamed. "You drunken sot! Get rid of that maniac friend of yours and go see Ralph—he's hurt!"

"Not for long," I said. "He'll be into our luggage before this thing is over."

She hung up and I turned to the bartender. "How old are you?" I asked him.

He tensed up, but said nothing.

I smiled at him. "You probably don't remember me," I said, "but I used to be the Governor." I offered him a Dunhill, which he declined.

"Governor of what?" he asked, dropping his hands to his sides, and turning to face us.

Skinner quickly stood up. "Let's have a drink for old times," he said to the bartender. "This gentleman was the Governor of American Samoa for ten years, maybe twenty."

"I don't remember him," said the bartender. "I get a lot of people in here."

Skinner laughed and slapped a twenty-dollar bill on the bar. "It's all bullshit anyway," he said. "We lie for a living, but we're good people."

He leaned over the bar and shook hands with the bartender, who was happy to see us leave. On the way to the lobby Skinner handed me a mimeographed copy of the Marathon schedule and said he'd meet us at the party. He waved cheerfully and signaled the bellboy to bring up his car.

Five minutes later, as I was still waiting for the elevator, I heard the nasty cold-steel roar of the GTO outside in the driveway, then the noise disappeared in the rain. The elevator came and I punched the button for the top floor.

HE WAS **NOT** **O**NE OF **U**S

Ralph was being massaged by an elderly
Japanese woman when his wife let me
into the suite. His eight-year-old daughter
was staring balefully at the TV set.

"Now you mustn't upset him," Anna warned
me. "He thinks his back is broken."

Ralph was in the bedroom, stretched out on a rubber
sheet and groaning piteously as the old crone pounded
his back. There was a bottle of Glenfiddich on the
sideboard and I made myself a drink. "Who was that
vicious thug you introduced me to in the lounge?"
he asked.

"That was Skinner," I said. "He's our contact for
the race."

"What?" he shouted. "Are you mad? He's a dope
addict! Did you hear what he said to me?"

"About what?" I asked.

"You heard him!" he yelled. "The White Death!"

"You should have offered him some," I said. "You
were rude."

"That was *your* work," he hissed at me. "*You* put
him up to it." He fell back on the rubber sheet, rolling
his eyes and baring his teeth at me, wracked by a
spasm of pain. "Damn you," he groaned. "Your
friends are *all* sick, and now you've picked up a
bloody dope addict!"

"Calm down, Ralph," I said. "They're all dope
addicts out here. We're lucky to meet a good one.
Skinner's an old friend. He's the official
photographer."

"Oh my God," he groaned. "I knew it would
be like this."

I looked over my shoulder to see if his wife was
watching, then I slapped him hard on the
temple, to bring him back to his senses.
He collapsed on the bed . . . and just at that
moment
Anna came into the room with a pot of tea and some
cups on a wicker tray that she'd ordered up from room service.

The tea calmed him down and soon he was talking normally.
The twelve-thousand-mile trip from London had been a fiendish
ordeal. His wife tried to get off the plane in Anchorage and
his daughter wept the whole way. The plane was struck twice
by lightning on the descent into Honolulu and a huge black

woman from Fiji who was sitting next to them had an epileptic seizure.

When they finally got on the ground, his luggage was lost and a cab charged him twenty-five pounds for a ride to the hotel, where their passports were seized by a desk clerk because he had no American money. The manager put the rest of his pounds in the hotel safe, for security, but allowed him to sign for snorkeling equipment at the surf shack on the beach by the Ho Ho Lounge.

He was desperate for refuge at this point, he said, wanting only to be alone, to relax by himself in the sea . . . so he put on his flippers and paddled out toward the reef, only to be picked up by a wave and bashed on a jagged rock, punching a hole in his spine and leaving him to wash up on the beach like a drowned animal.

"Strangers dragged me into a hut of some kind," he said. "Then they shot me full of adrenalin. By the time I could walk to the lobby I was pouring sweat and screaming. They had to give me a sedative and bring me up in the service elevator."

Only a desperate call to Wilbur had prevented the manager from having him committed to the jail ward of a public hospital somewhere on the other side of the island.

It was an ugly story. This was his first trip to the tropics, a thing he'd been wanting to do all his life . . . and now he was going to die from it, or at least be permanently crippled. His family was demoralized, he said. Probably none of them would ever get back to England, not even to be properly buried. They would die like dogs, for no good reason at all, on a rock far out in the middle of an utterly foreign sea.

The rain lashed against the windows as we talked. There was no sign of a break in the storm, which had been raging for many days. The weather was worse than Wales, he said, and the pain in his back was causing him to drink heavily. Anna cried every time he asked for more whiskey. "It's horrible," he said. "I drank a litre of Glenfiddich last night."

Ralph is always gloomy on foreign assignments. I examined his wound briefly and called down to the hotel gift shop for a ripe aloe plant.

"Send it up right away," I told the woman. "And we'll need something to chop it up with—do you have any big knives? Or a meat hatchet?"

There was no answer for a few seconds, then I heard sounds of shouting and scuffling, and a male voice came on the line. "Yes sir," he said, "were you asking about a weapon?"

I sensed at once that I was dealing with a businessman. The voice was Samoan, a deep croaking sound, but the instinct was universal Swiss.

"What do you have?" I asked him. "I need something to pulverize an aloe plant."

There was a pause, then he was back on the line.

"I have a fine cutlery set—seventy-seven pieces, with a beautiful butcher knife."

"I can get that from room service," I said. "What else do you have?"

There was another long pause. In the background I could hear a woman yelling something about "crazy . . ." and "chopping our heads off."

"You're fired," he screamed. "I'm tired of your stupid whining. It's none of your business what they buy. Get out of here! I should have fired you a long time ago!"

There were more sounds of brief scuffling and a babble of angry voices, then he was back.

"I think I have what you need," he said smoothly. "It's a carved Samoan war club. Solid ebony, with eight power points. You could pulverize a palm tree with it."

"How much does it weigh?" I asked.

"Well . . ." he said. "Ah . . . yes, of course, could you wait just a moment? I have a postage scale."

More noise came through the phone, a sharp rattling sound, then the voice.

"It's *very* heavy, sir. My scale won't handle it." He chuckled. "Yes sir, this thing is *heavy*. I'd guess about ten pounds. It swings like a sledgehammer. There's nothing in the world you couldn't kill with it."

"What's the price?" I asked.

"One-fifty."

"One-fifty?" I said. "For a stick?"

There was no reply for a moment. "No sir," he said finally. "This thing I have in my hands is not a *stick*. It's a Samoan war club, perhaps three hundred years old. It's also an extremely brutal weapon," he added. "I could break down your door with it."

"Never mind that," I said. "Send it up to the suite immediately, along with the aloe plant."

"Yes sir," he said. "And how should I bill it?"

"However you want," I said. "We're extremely rich people. Money means nothing to us."

"No problem," he said. "I'll be there in five minutes."

I hung up the phone and turned to Ralph, who was having another spasm, writhing soundlessly on the greasy rubber sheet. "It's all taken care of," I said. "We'll have you on your feet in no time. My man from the gift shop is coming up with an aloe plant and a vicious Samoan war club."

"Oh God!" he moaned. "Another one!"

"Yeah," I said, pouring myself another beaker of Glenfiddich. "He had that sound in his voice. We'll probably

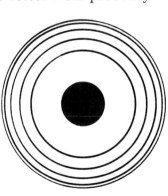

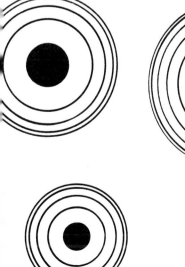

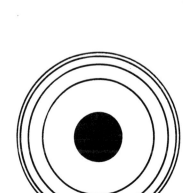

have to humor him." I smiled absently.
"We'll get into your stuff sooner or
later, Ralph. Why not right now?"
"What stuff?" he shouted.
"You know I don't use drugs."
"Come on, Ralph,"
I said. "I'm tired
of your hoary
lies, where
is it?"

Before he could answer there was a knock
on the door and a giant Samoan bounded into the
room, shouting "Aloha! Aloha!" and waving a huge
negro shinbone. "Welcome to the islands," he boomed.
"My name is Maurice. Here's your weapon."

It was an awesome thing to behold, easily capable of
smashing a marble toilet bowl.

"And here's a present." Maurice smiled, pulling a fat, ripe
marijuana pod out of his pocket. "There's plenty more where
this came from."

"Anna!" Ralph screamed. "Anna! Call the manager!"

I tapped Maurice on the shoulder and led him out to the
hall. "Mister Steadman is not himself today," I told him. "He
went snorkeling and broke his back on a coral head."

Maurice nodded. "Let me know if you need any help. I have
many relatives in Honolulu. I know many doctors."

"Me too," I replied. "I *am* a doctor."

We shook arms again and he bounded off toward the elevator.
I went back to the bedroom and pulverized the aloe plant,
ignoring Ralph's senile complaints. His wife watched nervously
as I carefully packed his wound with green mush. "There's
nothing wrong with his back," I told her. "It's only swollen.
He picked up some poison off the fire coral, but this aloe will
cure it."

Ralph passed out after the aloe treatment, but twenty minutes
later he was raving again and I persuaded him to eat a bag of
valerian root, which calmed his nerves instantly. The spasms
tapered off and he was able to sit up in bed and stare at the
evening news on TV, unfazed by scenes of hoodlums kicking
chunks of flesh off a tourist on a public beach near Pearl
Harbor. His eyes were dim and his face was sickly pale. Drops
of spittle ran down his chin. His speech was slow, and when I
told him about the limo that would be picking us up in three

hours to take us to a party, he seemed happy. "It will give us a chance to meet people," he said. "I want to make a deal with Budweiser."

I let it pass. That's the valerian root talking, I thought. Maybe I gave him too much.

He was drooling again, and his eyes were beginning to cross. He tried to roll a cigarette, but spilled tobacco all over the bed and I had to take the rolling machine away from him.

He seemed not to notice. "Is it still raining?" he muttered. "I can't stand this terrible weather. It's killing me."

"Don't worry," I said. "This is just a freak storm. All we have to do is have a look at this race, then get over to Kona and relax. The weather's fine over there."

He nodded, staring down through the heavy rain at a tiny red golf cart moving quietly along the fairway of the Wailalee Country Club.

"Kona?" he said finally. "I thought we were going to Guam, for the politics."

"What?"

"Guam," he said. "Some chap in Oregon rang me up . . ."

"That's Perry," I said. "From *Running*."

"That's right. The editor. He said we'd be off to Guam, to have a look at the bloody election."

"What?"

"Next Sunday."

"No, Ralph," I said finally. "The *Honolulu Marathon* is next Sunday. That's why we're here."

"Marathon?"

I stared at him. His teeth were jutting out of his mouth and his eyes were red slits in his face. The valerian root would be wearing off soon, but maybe not soon enough. In the meantime, he might die without some kind of stimulant.

I offered him the Glenfiddich bottle, which he eagerly grasped with both hands, whimpering softly as he raised it to his lips. He swallowed once, then uttered a low animal noise and vomited all over the bed.

I caught him as he was rolling off onto the floor and dragged him into the bathroom. He crawled the last few feet on his own, then collapsed on his knees in the shower stall.

I turned on the water, both knobs up to maximum, and closed the door so his wife and daughter wouldn't hear his degenerate screams.

The party that night was awkward. We arrived too late for dinner and there were "No Smoking" signs everywhere. Ralph tried to mingle, but he looked so sick that none of the guests would talk to him. Many were world-class runners, fanatics about personal health, and the sight of Ralph made them cringe. The aloe had half-cured his back, but he still walked like a stroke victim and his physical presence was not cheerful. He limped from room to room with his sketchbook, still deeply confused on valerian root, until a man wearing a silver Nike jumpsuit finally led him outside and said he should check himself into the leper colony on Molokai.

I found him leaning against the trunk of a monkeypod tree at the far end of the redwood deck, arguing bitterly with a stranger about the price of marijuana.

"It's a bloody awful habit," he was saying. "The smell of it makes me sick. I hope they put you in prison."

"You shiteating wino!" said the stranger. "It's people like you that give marijuana a bad name!"

Calorie Loading Party
Aloha Tower

I stepped quickly between them, dropping my full cup of beer on the deck. The stranger jumped back like a lizard and went into a karate crouch. "Don't touch me!" he shouted.

"You're going to prison," I said to him. "I warned you not to sell drugs to this man! Can't you see that he's sick?"

"What?" he screamed. Then he lunged at me, kicking savagely at my legs with a cleated running shoe. He missed and fell toward me, off balance, and I pushed my cigarette into his face as he staggered between us, slapping wildly at the fire on his chin.

"Get away!" I shouted. "We don't want any drugs! Keep your goddamn drugs to yourself!"

Others restrained the man as we hurried off. The limo was waiting at the top of the driveway. The driver saw us coming and started the engine, picking us up on the roll and careening out of the driveway with a long screech of rubber. Ralph had two spasms on the way to the hotel. The driver became hysterical and tried to flag down an ambulance at a stoplight on Waikiki Boulevard but I threatened to put a cigarette out on his neck unless we went straight to the hotel.

When we got there I sent the driver back to the party, to pick up the others. The Samoan night clerk helped me carry Ralph up to his room, then I ate two bags of valerian root and passed out.

We spent the next few days in deep research. Neither one of us had the vaguest idea what went on at a marathon, or why people ran in them, and I felt we should ask a few questions and perhaps mingle a bit with the runners.

This worked well enough, once Ralph understood that we were not going to Guam and that *Running* was not a political magazine. . . . By the end of the week we were hopelessly bogged down in a maze of gibberish about "carbo-loading," "hitting the wall," "the running divorce," "heel-toe theories," along with so many pounds of baffling propaganda about the Running Business that I had to buy a new Pierre Cardin seabag to carry it all.

We hit all the prerace events, but our presence seemed to make people nervous and we ended up doing most of our research in the Ho Ho Lounge at the Hilton. We spent so many hours talking to runners that I finally lost track of what it all meant and began setting people on fire.

It rained every day, but we learned to live with it . . . and by midnight on the eve of the race, we felt ready.

THE DOOMED GENERATION

We arrived at ground zero sometime around four in the morning—two hours before starting time, but the place was already a madhouse. Half the runners had apparently been up all night, unable to sleep and too cranked to talk. The air was foul with a stench of human feces and Vaseline. By five o'clock huge lines had formed in front of the bank of chemical privies set up

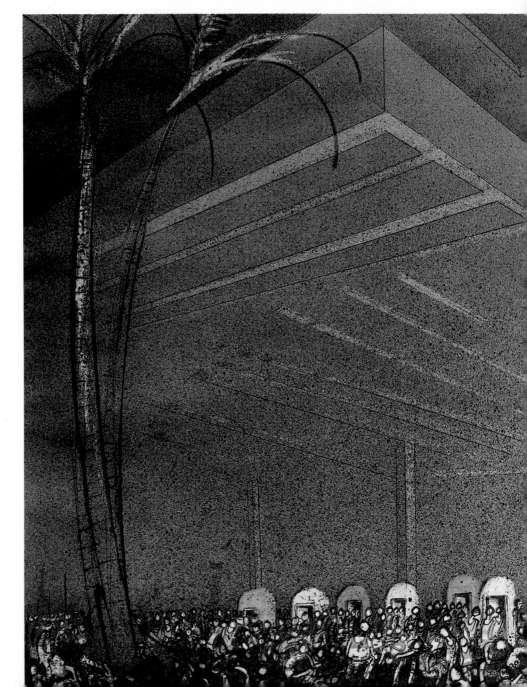

by Doc Scaff and his people. Prerace diarrhea is a standard nightmare at all marathons, and Honolulu was no different. There are a lot of good reasons for dropping out of a race, but bad bowels is not one of them. The idea is to come off the line with a belly full of beer and other cheap fuel that will burn itself off very quickly. . . .

Carbo-power. No meat. Protein burns too slow for these people. They want the starch. Their stomachs are churning like rat-bombs and their brains are full of fear.

Will they finish? That is the question. They want that "Finishers" T-shirt. Winning is out of the question for all but a quiet handful: Frank Shorter, Dean Matthews, Duncan MacDonald, Jon Sinclair.... These were the ones with the low numbers on their shirts: 4, 11, 16, and they would be the first off the line.

The others, the *Runners*—people wearing four-digit numbers— were lined up in ranks behind the Racers, and it would take them a while to get started. Carl Hatfield was halfway to Diamond Head before the big number people even tossed their Vaseline bottles and started moving, and they knew, even then, that not one of them would catch a glimpse of the winner until long after the race was over. Maybe get his autograph at the banquet....

We are talking about two very distinct groups here, two entirely different marathons. The Racers would all be finished and half drunk by 9:30 in the morning, or just about the time the Runners would be humping and staggering past Wilbur's house at the foot of "Heartbreak Hill."

At 5:55 we jumped on the tailgate of Don Kardong's KKUA radio press van, the best seats in the house, and moved out in front of the pack at exactly 11.5 miles per hour, or somewhere around the middle of second gear. The plan was to drop us off at Wilbur's house and then pick us up again on the way back.

Some freak with four numbers on his chest came off the line like a hyena on speed and almost caught up with our van and the two dozen motorcycle cops assigned to run interference . . . but he faded quickly.

We jumped off the radio van at Wilbur's and immediately set up a full wet-bar and Command Center next to the curb and for the next few minutes we just stood there in the rain and heaped every conceivable kind of verbal abuse on the Runners coming up.

"You're doomed, man, you'll never make it."

"Hey, fat boy, how about a beer?"

"*Run*, you silly bastard."

"Lift those legs."

"Eat shit and die," was Skinner's favorite.

One burly runner in the front ranks snarled back at him, "I'll see you on the way back."

"No, you won't. You'll never make it back. You won't even finish! You'll collapse."

It was a rare kind of freedom to belch any kind of cruel and brutal insult that came to mind because the idea of anybody stopping to argue was out of the question. Here was this gang of degenerates hunkered down by the side of the racecourse with TV sets, beach umbrellas, cases of beer and whiskey, loud music and wild women, smoking cigarettes.

It was raining—a light warm rain, but steady enough to keep the streets wet, so we could stand on the curb and hear every footfall on the pavement as the runners came by.

The front-runners were about thirty seconds behind us when we jumped off the still-moving radio van, and the sound of their shoes on the wet asphalt was not much louder than the rain. There was no sound of hard rubber soles pounding and slapping on the street. That noise came later, when the Racers had passed and the first wave of Runners appeared.

The Racers run smoothly, with a fine-tuned stride like a Wankel rotary engine. No wasted energy, no fighting the street or bouncing along like a jogger. These people *flow*, and they flow very fast.

The Runners are different. Very few of them flow, and not many run fast. And the slower they are, the more noise they make. By the time the four-digit numbers came by, the sound of the race was disturbingly loud and disorganized. The smooth rolling hiss of the Racers had degenerated into a hell broth of slapping and pounding feet.

We followed the race by radio for the next hour or so. It was raining too hard to stand out by the curb, so we settled down in the living room to watch football on TV and eat the big breakfast that Carol Wilbur had fixed "for the drunkards" before leaving at four in the morning to run in the Marathon. (She finished impressively, around 3:50.) It was just before eight when we got a call from Kardong in the radio van to be out on the curb for a rolling pickup on the way to the finish line.

Duncan MacDonald, a local boy and previous two-time winner, had taken command of the race somewhere around the 15-mile mark and was so far ahead that the only way he could lose this race would be by falling down—which was not likely, despite his maverick reputation and good-natured disdain for traditional training habits. Even drunk, he was a world-class racer, and a hard man for anybody to catch once he got out in front.

There was nobody near him when he passed the 24-mile mark in front of Wilbur's house, and we rode the final two miles to the finish line on the tailgate of the radio van, about 10 yards ahead of him . . . and when he came down the long hill from Diamond Head, surrounded by motorcycle cops and moving like Secretariat in the stretch at Churchill Downs, he looked about 10 feet tall.

"Jesus Christ," Skinner muttered. "Look at that bastard run."

Even Ralph was impressed. "This is beautiful," he said quietly, "this man is an *athlete*."

Which was true. It was like watching Magic Johnson run the fast break or Walter Payton turning the corner. A Racer in full stride is an elegant thing to see. And for the first time all week, the Running Business made sense to me. It was hard to imagine *anything* catching Duncan MacDonald at that point, and he was not even breathing hard.

We hung around the finish line for a while to watch the Racers coming in, then we went back to Wilbur's to have a look at the Runners. They straggled by, more dead than alive, for the rest of the morning and into the afternoon. The last of the finishers came in a few minutes after six, just in time to catch the sunset and a round of applause from the few rickshaw drivers still loitering in the park by the finish line.

Marathon running, like golf, is a game for *players*, not winners. That is why Wilson sells golf clubs, and Nike sells running shoes. The Eighties will not be a healthy decade for games designed only for winners—except at the very pinnacle of professional sport; like the Super Bowl, or the Heavyweight Championship of the World. The rest of us will have to adjust to this notion, or go mad from losing. Some people will argue, but not many. The concept of victory through defeat has already taken root, and a lot of people say it makes sense. The Honolulu Marathon was a showcase example of the New Ethic. The main prize in this race was a gray T-shirt for every one of the four thousand "Finishers." That was the test, and the only ones who failed were those who dropped out.

There was no special shirt for the winner, who finished so far ahead of the others that only a handful of them ever saw him until the race was long over . . . and not one of them was close enough to MacDonald, in those last two miles before the finish, to see how a real winner runs.

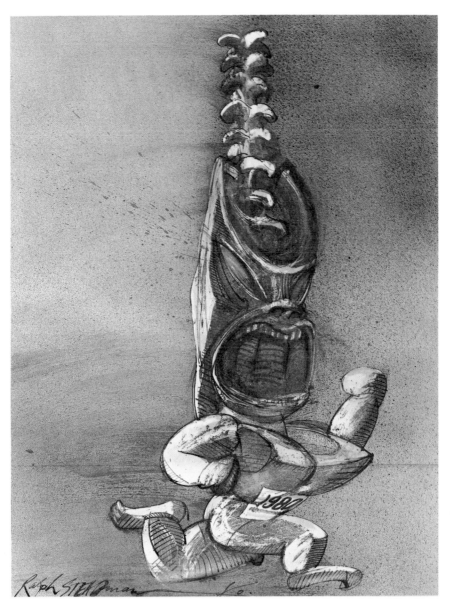

HITTING 'THE WALL
A Study.

The other five or six or even seven or eight thousand entrants were running for their own reasons . . . and *this* is the angle we need; the *raison d'être* as it were. . . . Why do those buggers run? Why do they punish themselves so brutally, for no prize at all? What kind of sick instinct would cause eight thousand supposedly smart people to get up at four in the morning and stagger at high speed through the streets of Waikiki for 26 ball-busting miles in a race that less than a dozen of them have the slightest chance of winning?

These are the kind of questions that can make life interesting for an all-expense-paid weekend at the best hotel in Honolulu. But that weekend is over now, and we have moved our base to Kona, 150 miles downwind—the "gold coast" of Hawaii, where anybody even half hooked in the local real estate market will tell you that life is better and bigger and lazier and . . . yes . . . even *richer* in every way than on any one of the other islands in this harsh little maze of volcanic zits out here in the middle of the Pacific Ocean, 5,000 miles from anywhere at all.

There's no sane reason at all for these runners. Only a fool would try to explain why four thousand Japanese ran at top speed past the USS *Arizona*, sunken memorial in the middle of Pearl Harbor, along with another four or five thousand certified American *liberals* cranked up on beer and spaghetti and all taking the whole thing so seriously that only one in two thousand could even smile at the idea of a 26-mile race featuring four thousand Japanese that begins and ends within a stone's throw of Pearl Harbor on the morning of December 7, 1980. . . .

Thirty-nine years later. What are these people celebrating? And why on this bloodstained anniversary?

It was a weird gig in Honolulu, and it is even weirder now. We are talking, here, about a thing with more weight than we know. What looked like a paid vacation in Hawaii has turned into a nightmare—and at least one person has suggested that we may be looking at the Last Refuge of the Liberal Mind, or at least the Last Thing that *Works.*

Run for your life, sport, because that's all you have left. The same people who burned their draft cards in the Sixties and got lost in the Seventies are now into *running.* When politics failed and personal relationships proved unmanageable; after McGovern went down and Nixon exploded right in front of our eyes . . . after Ted Kennedy got Stassenized and Jimmy Carter put the fork to everybody who ever believed anything he said about anything at all, and after the nation turned *en masse* to the atavistic wisdom of Ronald Reagan.

Well, these are, after all, the Eighties and the time has finally come to see who has teeth, and who doesn't. . . . Which may or may not account for the odd spectacle of two generations of political activists and social anarchists finally turning—twenty years later—into *runners.*

Why is this?

That is what we came out here to examine. Ralph came all the way from London—with his wife and eight-year-old daughter—to grapple with this odd question that I told him was vital but which in fact might mean nothing at all.

Why not come to Aspen and have some fun with the New Dumb?

Or why not skewer Hollywood? If only to get even with that scum. . . . Or even back to Washington, for the last act of "Bedtime for Bonzo"?

Why did we come all the way out here to what used to be called "the Sandwich Islands" to confront some half-wit spectacle like eight thousand rich people torturing themselves in the streets of Honolulu and calling it *sport?*

Well . . . there *is* a reason; or at least there *was*, when we agreed to do this thing.

The Fata Morgana.

Yes, *that* was the reason—some wild and elegant hallucination in the sky. We had both retired from journalism; then years

of working harder and harder for less and less money can make a man kinky. Once you understand that you can make more money by simply answering your telephone once a week than by churning out gibberish for the public prints at a pace keyed to something like three hours of sleep a night for thirty, sixty, or even eighty-eight hours in a stretch, it is hard to get up for the idea of going *back* into hock to American Express and Master Charge for just another low-rent look at what's happening.

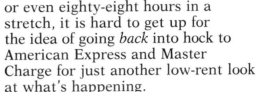

Journalism is a Ticket to Ride, to get personally involved in the same news other people watch on TV—which is nice, but it won't pay the rent, and people who can't pay their rent in the Eighties are going to be in trouble. We are into a very nasty decade, a brutal Darwinian crunch that will not be a happy time for free-lancers.

Indeed. The time has come to write *books*—or even movies, for those who can keep a straight face. Because there is money in these things; and there is no money in journalism.

But there *is action*, and action is an easy thing to get hooked on. It is a nice thing to know that you can pick up a phone and be off to anywhere in the world that interests you—on twenty-four hours notice, and especially on somebody else's tab.

That is what you miss: not the money, but the action—and that is why I finally drilled Ralph out of his castle in Kent for a trip to Hawaii and a look at this strange new phenomenon called "running." There was no good reason for it; I just felt it was time to get out in the world . . . get angry and tune the instruments . . . go to Hawaii for Christmas.

WHY DO THEY LIE TO US?

We fled Honolulu the next day, getting out just ahead
of a storm that closed the airport and cancelled
the surfing tournaments on the north shore.
Ralph was half crazy from the pain in his back and
the weather, but Wilbur assured him that Kona was
sunsoaked and placid.

The houses were all set and the agent, Mr. Heem, would meet
us at the airport. Uncle John would be over to see us in a few
days, with the family. Meanwhile take the sun and do some
diving out in front of the house, where the sea would be calm
as a lake.

Indeed. I was definitely ready for it—and even Ralph was
excited. The constant rain in Honolulu had broken his spirit,
and the wound on his spine was not healing. "You look sick," I
said to him as he staggered into the airport with a huge IBM
Selectric that he'd stolen from the hotel.

"I *am* sick," he shouted. "My whole body is rotting. Thank
God we're going to Kona. I *must* rest. I *must* see the *sun.*"

"Don't worry, Ralph," I said. "Wilbur's taken care of everything."

Which I believed at the time. He had no reason to lie, or at
least none I could see at the time.

It was ... as if the ships had by chance arrived at some
culmination in the lives of this community, a climax that
would affect their destiny. Polynesian excitement was one thing,
and they were familiar with that. In this bay the whole
population gave the impression of being on the brink of mass
madness. . . .

The canoes directed Cook's boat to Kealakekua village on the
eastern arm of the bay. As soon as they were ashore Cook, King
and Bayly were conscious of the silence by contrast with the
bedlam surrounding the ships. They were conscious, too, that the
atmosphere was quite different from any previous ceremony, as if
they were at the same time venerated yet restricted: half god, half
captive. Kanina took Cook firmly by the hand when they landed
on the volcanic rock shore and led him away as if he were his
prisoner. A native walked ahead of them incanting a dirge which
was repeated again and again. The word Lono was predominant,
and when the natives who had come out to greet them heard it
they prostrated themselves.

But he did. Almost everything he said was a lie. Our lives were about to become a living hell. Our Christmas would be a nightmare. Fear and loneliness would govern our lives, which would wander out of control. And we would all feel sicker and sicker every day. There would be no relief, no laughter; only craziness, despair and confusion.

Mr. Heem, the realtor, was waiting when we arrived at Kailua–Kona Airport, a palmy little oasis on the edge of the sea, about 10 miles out of town. The sun was getting low and there were puddles of water on the runway, but Mr. Heem assured us the weather was fine. "We'll sometimes get a little shower in the late afternoon," he said. "But I think you'll find it refreshing."

There was not enough room in his car for all our luggage, so I rode into town with a local fisherman called Captain Steve, who said he lived right up the beach from us. We loaded the luggage into his El Camino pickup and I sent the others on with Mr. Heem.

Ralph was agitated about leaving me alone with a stranger. "I can see it in his eyes," he said. "He's a dope addict. It's no accident that he was sitting here like a troll when we got off the plane."

"Ridiculous," I said. "He's picking up his girl friend. People are friendly over here, Ralph. It's not like Honolulu!"

"Oh God!" he moaned. "You're lying again. They're everywhere,

---

The party proceeded along the length of a wall of lava rocks, through the village, towards the *morai*, here called a *heiau*. It was huge and impressive, a rectangular black block set among the waving coconut trees and about 20 by 40 yards in size, surrounded by a fence in a state of disrepair on which were set 20 human skulls. Crudely carved grotesque wooden images grinning down at them from poles added to the threatening aspect of this holy place, which also featured an elaborate but dangerous looking scaffold with 12 more images set in a semi-circle, and a high altar upon which lay some sacrificial offerings, among them a lot of fruit and a huge half decayed hog.

Four natives had now appeared, ceremonially dressed and bearing wands tipped with dogs' hair, and chanting the word Lono.*

Richard Hough

The Last Voyage of Captain James Cook

*Or *Orono*, as Hough actually makes it out to be. "Orono" has been changed to Lono throughout.

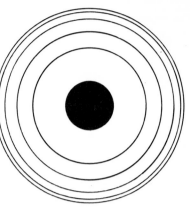

like pods—and you're one of them!"

"That's right," I said. "And so is this man Heem. He slipped me a package the minute we got off the plane."

He stared at me, then quickly pulled his daughter to his side. "It's horrible," he muttered. "Worse than perverts."

The highway from the airport into town was one of the ugliest stretches of road I'd ever seen in my life. The whole landscape was a desert of hostile black rocks, mile after mile of raw moonscape and ominous low-lying clouds. Captain Steve said we were crossing an old lava flow, one of the last eruptions from the 14,000-foot hump of Mauna Kea to our left, somewhere up in the fog. Far down to the right a thin line of coconut palms marked the new western edge of America, a lonely-looking wall of jagged black lava cliffs looking out on the white-capped Pacific. We were 2,500 miles west of the Seal Rock Inn, halfway to China, and the first thing I saw on the outskirts was a Texaco station, then a McDonald's hamburger stand.

Captain Steve seemed uneasy with my description of the estate he was taking me to. When I described the brace of elegant Japanese-style beach houses looking out on a black marble pool and a thick green lawn rolling down to a placid bay, he shook his head sadly and changed the subject. "We'll go out on my boat for some serious marlin fishing," he said.

"I've never caught a fish in my life," I said. "My temperament is wrong for it."

"You'll catch fish in Kona," he assured me as we rounded a corner into downtown Kailua, a crowded commercial district on the rim of the bay with half-naked people running back and forth through traffic like sand crabs.

We slowed to a crawl, trying to avoid pedestrians, but as we passed the Kona Inn a potbellied man with white hair carrying a beer bottle in each hand came running out of the driveway yelling, "You dirty bitch! I'll break your neck!" and crashed against the car at full speed, smacking my arm against the door. He fell back on the street and I tried to open the car door to get out and stomp on him, but my arm was completely numb. I couldn't lift it, or even move my fingers.

I was still in shock when we stopped at a red light and I noticed what appeared to be a cluster of garish-looking prostitutes standing in the shadows of a banyan tree on the sidewalk. Suddenly there was a woman leaning in my window, yelling gibberish at Captain Steve. She was trying to reach in and get

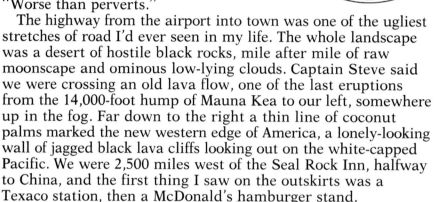

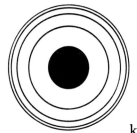

hold of him, but my arm was dead and I couldn't roll up the window. When she reached across me again I grabbed her hand and jammed my lit cigarette into her palm. The light changed and Captain Steve sped away, leaving the whore screeching on her knees in the middle of the intersection.

"Good work," he said to me. "That guy used to work for me. He was a first-class mechanic."

"What?" I said. "That whore?"

"That was no whore," he said. "That was Hilo Bob, a shameless transvestite. He hangs out on that corner every night, with all those other freaks. They're *all* transvestites."

I wondered if Mr. Heem had brought Ralph and his family along this same scenic route. I had a vision of him struggling desperately with a gang of transvestites in the middle of a traffic jam, not knowing what it meant. Wild whores with crude painted faces, bellowing in deep voices and shaking bags of dope in his face, demanding American money.

We were stuck in this place for at least a month, and the rent was $1,000 a week—half in advance, which we'd already paid Mr. Heem.

"It's a bad situation," Captain Steve was saying, as we picked up speed on the way out of town. "Those freaks have taken over a main intersection and the cops can't do anything about it." He swerved suddenly to avoid a pear-shaped jogger on the shoulder of the highway. "Hilo Bob goes crazy every time he sees my car," he said. "I fired him after he had a sex-change operation, so he got a lawyer and sued me for mental anguish. He wants a half-million dollars."

"Jesus," I said, still rubbing my wounded arm. "A gang of vicious bull fruits, harassing the traffic on main street."

"Yeah," he went on. "I made a real effort with Bob, but he got too weird for the clients. I'd get to the boat in the morning with a terrible hangover and find him asleep on the ice chest with his hair dyed orange and lipstick smeared all over his face. He got real bitchy and strange after he had his operation, and he started drinking a lot. I never knew what to expect. One morning he showed up with the ass cut out of his Levi's, but I didn't notice it until we were out of the harbor and I let him take the helm. I had a family of Japs on board, and they all went crazy at once. The grandfather was a famous fisherman, about ninety years old, and they'd brought him all the way to Kona

to catch his last marlin. I was up in the tower, still half sick
and asleep, when I heard a lot of screaming down in the cabin.
It sounded like Bob was being killed. I came down the ladder
with a loaded forty-five in my hand, and got hit in the face
with a spear handle by an old woman about four feet tall.
It knocked me out cold. By the time I woke up the boat
was running in circles and Bob was over the side,
fouled in the outrigger lines. He had two hooks in
his back and the water was full of blood, but they
wouldn't let me stop to pull him back aboard.
The old man wanted me to shoot him in the
water. I had to give them five hundred
dollars in cash before they let me pick
Bob up, then they stabbed him three
or four times on the way back

to port." He laughed bitterly. "It was the worst experience I've
ever had at sea. They reported me to the Coast Guard and I
almost lost my captain's license. The story was on the front
page of the newspaper. They charged me with sexual assault and
I had to defend myself at a public hearing." He laughed again.
"Jesus Christ! How do you explain a thing like that? The first
mate walking around the deck with the seat cut out of his
pants."

I said nothing. The story made me uncomfortable. What kind
of place had we come to? I wondered. And what if Ralph wanted
to go fishing? Captain Steve seemed okay, but the stories he
told were eerie. They ran counter to most notions of modern-
day sport fishing. Many clients ate only cocaine for lunch, he
said; others went crazy on beer and wanted to fight, on days
when the fish weren't biting. No strikes before noon put bad
pressure on the captain. For five hundred dollars a day, the
clients wanted big fish, and a day with no strikes at all could

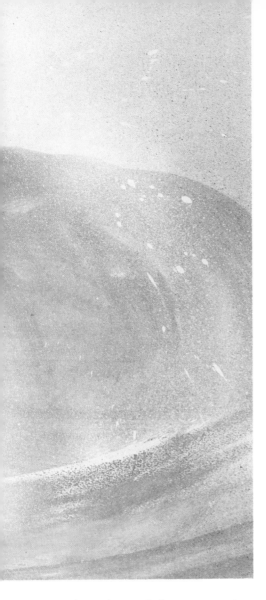

flare up in mutiny on the long ride back to the harbor at sunset. "You never know," he said. "I've had people try to put a gaffing hook into me, with no warning at all. That's why I carry the forty-five. There's no point calling the cops when you're twenty miles out to sea. They can't help you out there." He glanced in the direction of the surf, booming up on the rocks about a hundred yards to our right. The ocean was out there, I knew, but the sun had gone down and all I could see was blackness. The nearest landfall in that direction was Tahiti, 2,600 miles due south.

It was raining now, and he turned on the windshield wipers. We were cruising slowly along in bumper-to-bumper traffic. The highway was lined on both sides with what appeared to be unfinished apartment buildings, new condominiums and raw construction sites littered with bulldozers and cranes. The roadside was crowded with long-haired thugs carrying surfboards, paying no attention to traffic. Captain Steve was getting edgy, but he said we were almost there.

"It's one of these hidden driveways," he muttered, slowing down to examine the numbers on a row of tin mailboxes.

"Impossible," I said. "They told me it was far out at the end of a narrow country road."

He laughed, then suddenly hit the brakes and swung right through a narrow slit in the shrubbery beside the road. "This is it," he said, jamming the brakes again to keep from running up on the back of Mr. Heem's car. It was parked with all the doors open in a cluster of cheap wooden shacks about 15 feet off the highway. There was nobody in sight, and the rain was getting dense. We quickly loaded the baggage out of the El Camino and into the nearest shack, a barren little box with only two cots and a Salvation Army couch for furniture. The sliding glass doors looked out on the sea, like they said, but we were afraid to open them, for fear of the booming surf. Huge waves crashed down on the black rocks in front of the porch. White foam lashed the glass and water ran into the living room, where the walls were alive with cockroaches.

The storms continued all week: murky sun in the morning, rain in the afternoon and terrible surf all night. We couldn't even swim in the pool, much less do any diving. Captain Steve was becoming more and more frantic about our inability to get in the water, or even go near it. We conferred each day on the phone, checking the weather reports and hoping for a break.

The problem, he explained, was an off-shore storm somewhere out in the Pacific—maybe a hurricane on Guam, or something worse down south around Tahiti. In any case, something we couldn't control or even locate was sending big rollers across the ocean from some faraway place. Hawaii is so far out in the middle of nothing that a mild squall in the straits of Malacca, 3,000 miles away, can turn a six-inch ripple into a sixteen-foot wave by the time it hits Kona. There is no other place in the world that so consistently bears the brunt of other people's weather.

The Kona Coast is on the leeward side of the Big Island, protected by the towering humps of two 14,000-foot volcanoes from the prevailing northeast winds. The whole east coast of the island is a jagged wasteland of ferns and black boulders, lashed by the same Arctic winds that make the north coast of Oahu a surfer's paradise.

But the same wave that picks up a surfboard can also pick up a boat and send it rocketing toward the beach at terrible speeds. Nobody who has ever taken that ride wants to do it again. "There's no way you can ride it out," Captain Steve told me. "If you try to keep it straight you'll get smashed on the rocks like some kind of flying egg—and if you try to turn out of the wave, the boat will broach and start rolling. Either way, you're doomed."

It happened to a friend of his once, he said. "He was coming in with a party of tourists one afternoon. They were in an ugly mood because nobody had caught a fish, so he was keeping an eye on them and talking to his wife on the radio at the same time, not watching the waves—when all of a sudden he realized he was ten feet out of the water and coming into the harbor so fast that all he could do was jump. The boat kept on going and he said he could hear those poor bastards screaming all the way into the rocks." He smiled ruefully. "One guy was down below changing his pants when the boat finally flipped; he was trapped in an air pocket under the boat for two hours before we could get him out. We had to come up underneath him with tanks, then get hold of his legs and drag him down about eighteen

We hear all our lives about the "gentle, stormless Pacific," and about the "smooth and delightful route to the Sandwich Islands," and about the "steady blowing trades," that never vary, never change, never "chop around," and all the days of our boyhood we read how that infatuated old ass, Balboa, looked out from the top of a high rock upon a broad sea as calm and peaceful as a sylvan lake, and went into an ecstasy of delight, like any other greaser over any other trifle, and shouted in his foreign tongue and waved his country's banner, and named his great discovery "Pacific"— thus uttering a lie which will go on deceiving generation after generation of students while the old ocean lasts. If I had been there, with my experience, I would have said to this man Balboa, "Now, if you think you have made a sufficient display of yourself, cavorting around on this conspicuous rock, you had better fold up your old rag and get back into the woods again, because you have jumped into a conclusion, and christened this sleeping boy-baby with a girl's name, without stopping to inquire into the sex of it."

From all that I can discover, if this foreign person had named this ocean the "Four Months Pacific," he should have come nearer the mark. My information is to the effect that the summer months give fine weather, smooth seas, and steady winds, with a month and a few days good weather at the far end of spring and the beginning of autumn and that the other seven or eight months of the year one can calculate pretty regularly on head winds and stern winds, and winds on the quarter, and winds several points aloft the beam, and winds that blow straight up from the bottom, and still other winds that come so straight down from above that the fore-stuns'l-spanker-jib-boom makes a hole through them as clean as a telescope. And the sea rolls and leaps and chops and surges "thortships" and up and down and fore-and-aft by turns, when the gales are blowing; and when they die out, the old nor'west swell comes in and takes a hand, and stands watch, and keeps up the marine earthquake until the winds are rested and ready to make trouble again.

In a word, the Pacific is "rough" for seven or eight months in the year—not stormy, understand me; not what one could just call stormy, but contrary, baffling, and very "rough."

Therefore, if that Balboa-constrictor had constructed a name for it that had "Wild" or "Untamed" to it, there would have been a majority of two months in the year in favor and in support of it.

Mark Twain

Letters from Hawaii

feet before we could take him up." He shook his head, no longer smiling. "Jesus," he said, "I hope I never have to see a thing like that again. He was stark naked and completely hysterical by the time we got him to the dock. It was a terrible scene. The whole crowd was laughing at him, and that made him even crazier. One of the guys who tried to help him out of the dinghy still has teeth marks all over his arm. Then he locked himself in a car and we had to break a window to get him out.

"The boat was a total loss," he added. "Probably fifty or sixty thousand dollars. What was left of it finally sank and blocked the entrance to the harbor for five days."

Waves like that are rare on the Kona Coast, where the waters are usually more placid than anywhere else in the islands— except when the weather turns around, as they say, and the winds blow in from the west.
Mark Twain did not lie—at least not about the Pacific Ocean in winter. The Kona Coast in December is as close to hell on earth as a half-bright mammal can get—and this is the *leeward* side of the "Big Island": this is the *calm* side.

God only knows what happens over there on the windward side, around Hilo. . . . That is the "wet coast," they say, and even real estate agents will warn you against going over *there*, for any reason at all.

But they will *not* warn you about Kona . . . so that will have to be my job; for as long as the grass is green and the rivers flow to the sea. The Kona Coast of Hawaii might be a nice place to visit for a few hours on the hottest day in July—but not even fish will come near this place in the winter; if the surf doesn't kill you, the Surge will, and anybody who tries to tell you anything different should have his teeth gouged out with a chisel.

ALOHA from HAWAII.

HST: *I'm calling about a wave warning I just heard on the radio. We're visiting out here, tourists in fact.*

COP: *Yeah—where you staying at?*

HST: *I'm out past Magic Sands.*

COP: *Right on the beach?*

HST: *Right smack on the beach.*

COP: *Okay—we are expecting high surf about four o'clock this morning.*

HST: *What does this mean to me? We've had some pretty high surf out here.*

COP: *Yeah, well, it means it's going to possibly crest at seventeen feet this morning at about four.*

HST: *Seventeen feet? Is that measuring* behind *the wave? That's actually—ah—that's a real high sea, isn't it?*

COP: *Right. Something about a storm to the north of the islands or whatever. However, right now, they're only advising. But if there's any loose gear, it should be secured.*

HST: *Is this going to pick rocks out of the ocean and put them into my bedroom?*

COP: *No, not quite that bad we hope. Ah—of course if it worsens, if the situation worsens, the CD, the Civil Defense will become involved.*

HST: *Well, if it's four o'clock in the morning most of us will be asleep, hopefully. How will we know when it gets serious?*

COP: *Well, we'll probably use some police cars or the fire department with loudspeakers and go down Alii Drive recommending evacuation. But right now it's just an advisory.*

HST: *This is that same storm from the North? And it's going to get* worse?

COP: *At four this morning the high tides will be at their worst.*

HST: *The worst.*

COP: *Right. But right now it appears fairly calm.*

HST: *It does. I was just downtown —it looked very calm to me.*

COP: *The waves in Kailua Bay are running five feet; Kaheo Bay, nothing—no wave action at all.*

HST: *What was the size of the waves we had about two weeks ago? That's when we had some trouble up here. They came up to the porch.*

COP: *I really don't know, I wasn't working at that time, apparently, because I don't recall it.*

HST: *There was no alert. It wasn't that high. Maybe eight or ten feet—I was just trying to compare. Well, we'll see, won't we?*

COP: *Yeah, as I said, right now they're just advising if you have any gear on your back porch or whatever, make sure it's secure.*

HST: (laughs) *Secure. . . .*

COP: *And they will take steps to alert the populace near the beach.*

HST: *Steps? What kind of steps? Phone calls? Sirens? How will we know? Like I said, we'll probably be asleep.*

COP: *Well, as I said, they'll either use the loudspeakers on the police cars and fire department vehicles or they'll be using—*(PAUSE)*—they'll be using the Civil Defense siren—which will wake you up, guaranteed.*

HST: *Okay, but we won't be taken out of our beds by a tsunami?*

COP: *No tsunami. Don't worry about that.*

HST: *Okay, thank you.*

COP: *You're welcome. Bye.*

TITS LIKE ORANGE FIREBALLS

All work ceased on my side of the compound as the holiday season approached. I hunkered down for the pro football playoffs, betting heavily with Wilbur on the telephone and squandering away my winnings on fireworks. The Christmas season, in Hawaii, is also the time of the annual Feast of Lono, the god of excess and abundance. The missionaries may have taught the natives to love Jesus, but deep in their pagan hearts they don't really like him: Jesus is too stiff for these people. He had no sense of humor. The ranking gods and goddesses of the old Hawaiian culture are mainly distinguished by their power, not their purity, and they are honored for their vices as well as their awesome array of virtues. They are not intrinsically different from the people themselves—just bigger and bolder and better in every way.

The two favorites are Lono and Pele, the randy Volcano goddess. When Pele had a party, *everybody* came; she was a lusty long-haired beauty who danced naked on molten lava with a gourd of gin in each hand, and anybody who didn't like it was instantly killed. Pele had her problems—usually with wrong-headed lovers, and occasionally with whole armies—but in the end she always prevailed. And she still lives, they say, in her cave underneath a volcano on Mt. Kiluea and occasionally comes out to wander around the island in any form she chooses—sometimes as a beautiful young girl on a magic surfboard, sometimes a jaded harlot sitting alone at the bar of the Volcano House; but usually—for some reason the legends have never made clear—in the form of a wizened old woman who hitchhikes around the island with a pint of gin in her kitbag.

Whether Pele and Lono ever got together is a question still shrouded in mystery, but as a gambler I would have to bet on it. There is not enough room on these islands for the two most powerful deities in Hawaiian history to roam around for 1,000 years without coming to grips with each other.

King Lono, ruler of all the islands in a time long before the Hawaiians had a written language, was not made in the same mold as Jesus, although he seems to have had the same basically decent instincts. He was a wise ruler and his reign is remembered in legend as a time of peace, happiness and great abundance in the kingdom—the Good Old Days, as it were, before the white man came—which may have had something to do with his elevation to the status of a god in the wake of his disappearance.

Lono was also a chronic brawler with an ungovernable temper, a keen eye for the naked side of life and a taste for strong drink at all times. This side of his nature, although widely admired by his subjects, kept him in constant trouble at home. His wife, the lovely Queen Kaikilani Alii, had a nasty temper of her own, and the peace of the royal household was frequently shattered by monumental arguments.

It was during one of these spats that King Lono belted his queen across the hut so violently, at least once, that he accidentally killed her. Kaikilani's death plunged him into a fit of grief so profound that he abandoned his royal duties and took to wandering around the islands, staging a series of boxing and wrestling matches in which he took on all comers. But he soon tired of this and retired undefeated, they say, sometime around the end of the eighth or ninth century. Still bored and distraught, he then took off in a magic canoe for a tour of "foreign lands"—from whence he would return, he promised, as soon as the time was right.

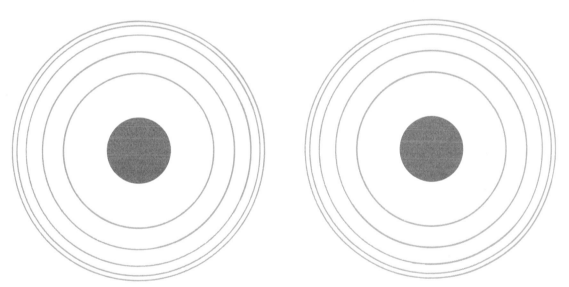

The natives have been waiting for this moment ever since, handing his promise down from one generation to another and faithfully celebrating the memory of their long-lost God/King at the end of each year with a two-week frenzy of wild parties and industrial-strength fireworks. The missionaries did everything in their power to wean the natives away from their faith in what amounted to a kind of long-overdue alter-Christ, and modern politicians have been trying for years to curtail or even ban the annual orgy of fireworks during the Christmas season, but so far nothing has worked.

THERE **A**RE **NO** **R**ULES

We learned these things—or at least a few of them—
from Captain Steve, the local charter fisherman
who befriended us when we arrived at the
Kailua–Kona Airport and subsequently became our
main man on the island. Captain Steve had a fully-
rigged fishing boat and was determined to take us out and catch
a marlin—a gesture of fine hospitality that promised to make
our stay in Kona even richer and more exciting than we'd known
it was going to be, all along. Wilbur also had a fishing trip
lined up for us; and Stan Dzura, an old friend from Colorado,
had a boat that he'd offered to let us use any time we wanted.

It had seemed up to that point, that we were definitely in good
shape, and as the winter solstice approached I felt optimistic
enough to invite my son, Juan, over to Hawaii for a week or so
of the finest water sport. The Kona Coast is one of the world's
best game-fishing grounds, regarded by serious anglers as the
equal of anything to be found in the Bahamas or the Great
Barrier Reef in Australia.

Both Ralph and I were pleased at our unexpected run of high
luck. In addition to having our own pool and a private beach
right in front of the compound for swimming and skin diving,
now we also had our own boats to get out on the ocean and stalk
the mighty marlin. Money was no problem, Captain Steve
explained. Charter boats in Kona normally go for $500 a day,
but for us that fee would be waived; all we had to do was
bring our own food and drink. . . .

Indeed. Just the sight of these words on paper sends a shudder
up my spine even now, long after we finally escaped and moved
on to other ordeals. We will get to the details later, but the
main bearings of the story and all we need to know for now are
these: 1) Early in December we moved into a kind of seaside
estate containing a pool and three wooden houses—one for the
caretaker, one for Ralph and his family, and another for me,
Laila and Juan. 2) Captain Steve, who lived not far up the beach
from us, became more and more obsessed with getting us out
on the sea to catch fish. 3) In December of that year the Kona
Coast was lashed by a series of terrible storms that made our
lives a living hell. And 4) our social behavior turned so ugly
and rude that we were shunned by the natives and eventually
turned to excessive use of fireworks, whiskey and bad craziness
in the compound.

The Kona fishing fleet stayed safely in port during this period,
leaving Captain Steve and the other seafaring types with a lot
of time on their hands—which most of them spent on barstools,

bitching endlessly about the weather, the dearth of paying tourists on the island and the first bad signs of what some of them saw as the imminent collapse of the local real estate market. Hawaii had been the only state in the Union that didn't vote for Reagan, so there were a lot of people hanging idly around the bars who kept saying "I told you so" to anybody who would listen.

This was the situation we found ourselves mired in, and the only escape—for me, at least—was watching football on television, which I did with a zeal that got more and more on Ralph's nerves. His lifelong hatred of sport made it impossible for him to share my preoccupation with gambling on the games, and we slowly drifted apart—he to his kinky brooding, and me to the TV set, usually far up the mountain at Stan Dzura's house. On the few occasions when we all went into town together, Ralph's eccentric behavior so offended the natives that some called him "the queer" and others called him "Wolfman." By the time we had been there two weeks he was known everywhere we went as "The Queer and Famous Wolfman," and he was not much fun to be with.

One by one, we all got off the boat. Ralph went first, as always—and, as always, he blamed it on me. Which was true, in a way. The whole thing *was* my fault. It was *my* plan that had gone wrong, not Ralph's, and now his whole family was in the throes of a profound psychotic experience. Some people can handle ten days in the eye of a hurricane, and some can't.

Ralph was becoming more and more concerned about this aspect of our situation, as it daily became more desperate. His primitive Welsh ancestry would allow him to cling almost indefinitely to his own sanity, he felt, but he was not confident about the ability of his wife or young daughter to survive a shock of this magnitude. "How many days of abject terror can an eight-year-old girl endure?" he asked me one day as we shared a pint of hot gin in his kitchen. "I can already see the signs. She's withdrawing into herself, gnawing on balls of twine and talking to cockroaches at night."

"That's why we have insane asylums," I said. "When your neighbors start talking about their children at Oxford or Cambridge, you can brag that you have a daughter in Bedlam."

He stiffened, then shook it off and laughed harshly. "That's right," he said. "I can visit her on weekends, invite all my neighbors to attend her graduation."

We were half mad ourselves, at this point. All of our desperate efforts to flee the Big Island had come to naught. We couldn't even get seats on a plane back to Honolulu, much less to anywhere else. . . . And our Will to Flee was *real:* I would have written a bad check for a charter jet to Tahiti, 2,600 miles, one way—but the storm had knocked out our telephones and there was no hope of getting through to anybody more than a mile or two away. The only place we could be sure of reaching was the bar at the Kona Inn.

The long and tedious ceremony and feast were at last over, and Cook indicated that they would like to set up an encampment at the *heiau*. Chiefs Parea and Kanina understood at once, and when Cook selected a walled field of sweet potatoes, with many assurances of compensation for the owner, the priests stuck their wands on the wall to consecrate and "taboo" it.

They now returned to their boat and as they passed through the village, Cook in his red cloak, men, women and children all dropped onto their knees and lay with their heads to the ground until they had passed. Lono! . . . Lono! . . .

What he did not know, and never did learn, was that he had been acknowledged as the incarnation of the god Lono. His arrival was the greatest event in Hawaii's history. *Lono makua* was the Hawaiian god of the season of abundance and relaxation, who was said to process clockwise about the island to be greeted by white banners and elaborate ceremonies of obeisance. Cook had arrived, at the appointed time, and by reason of his decision to sail slowly offshore for better trading, had indeed progressed slowly and clockwise about the island, his standard at his masthead a divine acknowledgement of the white banners ashore. And properly, and according to tradition, he had come to rest at Kealakekua, "the path of the gods," in his miracle giant canoe opposite the *heiau* in the middle of the god's season, in time for the great ceremonies of worship annually accorded to him for the abundance of riches he caused the soil to grant them.

Cook may have been late for the Arctic summer but the timing of his arrival off Hawaii could not be faulted. His subsequent actions did have a near-divine verisimilitude, and the climax had now been reached with the ceremonies he had just undergone. Everything that he experienced over the following two weeks conformed with the legend of the god Lono. It is little wonder that his reception—"this remarkable homage" as King described it—here at Hawaii was so different from that at any other Polynesian island, and that the natives had been thrown into a state of near-hysteria. Not even the oldest citizen with the longest memory could recall hearing from his oldest ancestor of the appearance in incarnated form of the great god Lono.

Richard Hough

The Last Voyage of Captain James Cook

TRAPPED IN A QUEER PLACE

It is Monday night on the Kona Coast, two days before Christmas. Three o'clock in the morning. No more Monday night football. The season is over. No more Howard Cosell and no more of that shiteating lunatic with the rainbow-striped afro wig. That freak should be put to sleep, and never mind the reasons. We don't need that kind of craziness out here in Hawaii, not even on TV . . . and especially not now, with the surf so high and wild thugs in the streets of Waikiki and this weather so foul for so long that people are starting to act crazy. A lot more people than normal for this time of year are going to flip out, if we don't see the sun by Christmas.

They call it "Kona Weather"; gray skies and rough seas, hot rain in the morning and mean drunks at night, bad weather for coke fiends and boat people. . . . A huge ugly cloud hangs over the island at all times, and this goddamn filthy sea pounds relentlessly up on the rocks in front of my porch. . . . The bastard never sleeps or even rests; it just keeps coming, rolling, booming, slamming down on the rocks with a force that shudders the house every two or three minutes.

I can feel the sea in my feet as I sit here and type, even in those moments of nervous quiet that usually mean a Big One is on its way, gathering strength out there in the darkness for another crazed charge on the land.

My shirt is damp with a mixture of sweat and salt spray. My cigarettes bend like rubber and the typing paper is so limp that we need waterproof pens to write on it . . . and now that evil white foam is coming up on my grass, just six feet away from the porch.

This whole lawn might be halfway to Fiji next week. Last winter's Big Storm took the furniture off every porch on this stretch of the coast and hurled boulders the size of TV sets into people's bedrooms. Half the lawn disappeared overnight and the pool filled up with rocks so big that they had to be lifted out with a crane.

Our pool is a lot closer to the sea now. On the night we arrived I was almost sucked into the surf by a wave that hit while I was standing on the diving board, and the next day an even bigger one rolled over the pool and almost killed me.

We stayed away from the pool for a few days, after that. It makes a man queasy to swim laps in a pool where the sea might *come and get you* at any moment, with no warning at all. It is like getting hit by a moeter (moeter). Meptpr? Meotor? Meteor . . . yes that sounds right: like getting hit by a meteor while driving to work on the freeway.

Ralph is hunkered down next door in a state of abject terror.

The whole family is sleeping on the living room floor with all their baggage packed and ready to flee for their lives on a moment's notice. When I tried to get in and steal Ralph's TV for the late basketball game I almost stepped on the child's head as I came over the edge of that slimy wooden porch.

Why do they lie to us?

That is what haunts me now, the weird fishhook in this story that keeps me from just leaping on it like some kind of brute on the run coming up on a high-polished brass fire pole and suddenly . . . . yes, a way out. .

Zoom. . . . Grab the pole, through the floor, out of sight, big black rubber pad at the bottom. And after that, run like a bastard and never look back . . . because whatever's after you is probably in better shape than you are, and it probably won't slow down.

Those buggers run 26 consecutive five-minute miles. But not even that is fast enough to stay ahead of that thing that keeps gaining. . . .

Why don't they ride motorcycles?

Why indeed?

We will have to deal with that later, for good or ill.

All we know, for now, and all we need to know, is that this goddamn rotten surf is still thundering up on the lawn at five in the morning and this dirty Hawaiian nightmare has been going on for thirteen straight days.

BOMB FEVER

After two weeks on the Kona Coast I found myself looking for stray dogs to run over, every time I drove into town . . . and the drunker I got, the more dogs I wanted to kill.

The only other thing that makes sense is *bombs*, and we reached that point in Kona on Christmas Eve. Here is a wild scrawl that I found on a page in my notebook, dated December 25:

This filthy goddamn sea is still raging and pounding on the rocks in front of my porch. Somewhere to the west is a monster storm of some kind, with 40-knot winds and 35-foot seas. That is a <u>typhoon</u> I think. We are paying $1,000 a week to sit out here in the rain on the edge of this savage black rock and wait for the annual typhoon—like the fools they know us to be.

Well, fuck these people. They lied to us, and their lies have caused us to suffer . . . which means we must go to the mattresses and bomb them into the sea. We've been crouched like dumb wet animals in this place for fifteen days now, and that's at least ten too many. We are living on the edge of the sea, but we can't go near the water. To dive off those rocks in front of the houses would mean instant death. Fifty feet in front of my typewriter is a living thundering hell of white foam and riptides and huge blasts of spray that not even a shark could survive in. The time has come for vengeance.

The time came yesterday in fact. We finally got weird enough, around midnight on Christmas Eve, to set off a huge Chinese bomb on the front porch of a local charter fisherman's house. It went off with a genuinely terrifying blast about three-tenths of a second after I put the match to the fuse.

I have set off a lot of firecrackers, but nothing I've ever lit had a kick like this bastard. I tried to run, but the fuse was so quick that I was only a step and a half into my stride when suddenly the whole world turned bright scorching yellow and I was tumbling around in the bushes about ten feet across the driveway. I wound up on my knees, with all the hair burned off my legs, staring back at the house as it disappeared in the eye of a wild fireball that I remember thinking at the time would be the last thing I'd ever see.

This thing was no firecracker; it was a flat-out Bomb—2,490 bright red Chinese firecrackers packed into a 10-pound lump and nicely wrapped with a time-release fuse that makes the explosion seem to go on forever. Most firecrackers explode and die instantly, but this thing went off like God's own drumroll . . . and it *kept* going off, and it kept getting louder, until finally I got The Fear. The noise was too intense, and the fireball was getting bigger; the porch seemed to be coming apart in very slow motion, and I heard a scream from inside.

There were two of them in there, and the eerie pitch of that scream told me that one had already gone mad—while the bomb was still happening—and the thought of it filled me with horror. I was slumped on my knees in the driveway, so close to the edge of the fireball that I knew it would make me blind if I kept my eyes open—but I couldn't close them; I was paralyzed with awe, by this terrible thing I had wrought.

This is not what I meant, I thought. Not what I meant at all. It was supposed to be a joke, a symbolic gesture of sorts . . . the time had come, I felt, to reestablish the ancient Hawaiian "Law of the Splintered Oar."

The Law of the Splintered Oar

At the time—before Hawaii was unified—a series of inter-island wars prevailed among rival chiefs. King Kamehameha I, himself, made a series of destructive and senseless raids upon peaceful coasts and people. In one of these raids, he attacked some fishermen, and in return, one man hit Kamehameha on the head with an Oar. The force was so great that a second blow would have been fatal. Later, when the fisherman was captured and brought before Kamehameha, he did not kill the man, but admitted that his own attack had been wrong, and that all such wanton attacks were wrong. As a result, the Law of the Splintered Oar came into being, providing protection for peaceful citizens from raids and senseless pillaging by rival chiefs.

The notion had come to me fast, as good notions will, and I immediately went to the phone. It was eleven o'clock on Christmas Eve, our fourteenth day on this foggy, surf-whipped rock, and life was getting tense. But nobody had lied to me for three or four hours and I was just into the second stage of trying to relax, when all of a sudden the drunken caretaker veered into some kind of sleazy rap about selling me a tin boat that he had stashed on a bay somewhere in Alaska, for $12,000—so I could fish in the ocean for herring and make $50,000 a day.

Once I had the boat (along with a "permit"—another $60 up front) I could go out with the fleet and drop my net with the others. Right. And for the next three weeks we would stay awake twenty-four hours a day, ram-feeding each other with handfuls of speed and hauling constantly on the nets.

"We get a little crazy out there," he said, "but it's worth it. Fifty thousand dollars a day!"

I nodded and stared out to sea, feeling the bile rise. Jesus, I thought, these people *have no shame*. First the Kona Coast, and now a herring scam in Alaska. On Christmas Eve, for $12,000 cash. . . .

I stood up suddenly. "Okay," I said. "The joke's over. It's time for the bomb."

"What?" he said, "you want a bomb?"

"I *have* a bomb," I said. "I have six goddamn bombs and a long white beard and these lies are driving me *mad*! Where's the phone?"

He pointed, and I dialed the first number that came into my head. It was Captain Steve, who had taken us out on his boat the day before and caught no fish. No fish at all—which was not a surprise to me, but Ralph took it hard. They had strapped him into the fighting chair at dawn, facing backwards into our wake and a thick fog of diesel fumes; then they put a gigantic rod and reel in his lap and told him to hang on, because the bait he was trailing would be swallowed at any moment by a fish the size of a bull moose, which would then erupt from the deep like a missile and "take off across the top of the water at seventy miles an hour."

Ralph nodded solemnly as we tightened the straps. "Well, well," he said. "That's bloody *fast*, I'd say."

I laughed. "Don't worry, Ralph, it's all bullshit. We won't catch a fucking thing."

He smiled nervously. "That's a bloody fast fish," he muttered. "Seventy miles an hour on the surface? And you say it's the size of a bull?" He glanced down at the reel in his hand. "Do we have the proper equipment?"

"Damn right," said Captain Steve. "Just be sure to keep your hands off the reel when he takes off. That line will go out so fast that the reel will get hot enough to explode in your hands, like a bomb."

The fish never happened.

But the bomb did. It was nothing personal, but I felt it had to be done. . . .

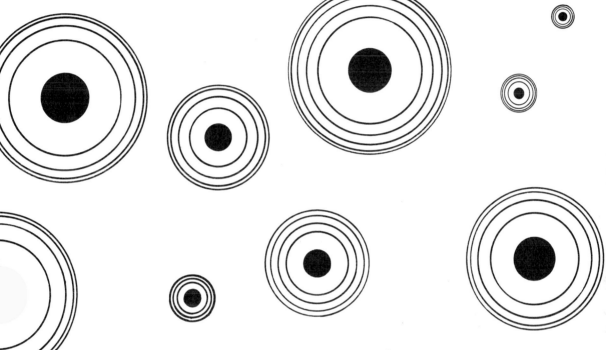

Ralph and his family had never been west of San Francisco and the only palm tree they'd ever seen was on the Universal lot in Hollywood. . . . But now, as Christmas approached, they found themselves marooned in a wooden shack on the edge of some barren wave-whipped black rock in the middle of the Pacific Ocean, with nobody speaking their language and estranged from even their closest friends.

The British are very sentimental about Christmas. They want the snow and the slush of England, diseased beggars ringing bells on every street corner, news of food riots on the telly, the familiar sickening chill of a stone home with no furnace and the family huddled cheerfully around a pot of burning coal on Christmas morning. They are not comfortable with the idea of Saint Nick coming in on a surfboard with a sack full of cockroaches and a *TV Guide* filled with nothing but incomprehensible American "football" games for the next two weeks.

Some days later Cook learned that the king of Hawaii, no less, had arrived at Kealakekua and was to visit him. James King was at this time stationed ashore in command of the encampment to ensure its security. He had had no troubles at all from the natives. The natives would sometimes sit on the wall watching the incomprehensible activities of Bayly and his assistants and the impressive activities of the carpenters with their wonderful tools that could work timber with such seeming ease and accuracy.

The escorting chiefs, dressed in elaborate cloaks and hats, began to sing as they approached the Resolution, chanting with great solemnity, and then standing up. As they came near, the reception party on board observed that the second canoe held also High Priest Koa, hunched and shaking as always, elaborately attired and surrounded by hideous busts made of basketwork. These were covered with multicolored feathers, the eyes represented by pearl oyster shell, the distorted mouths filled with the teeth of dogs.

The king himself remained seated when his canoe came alongside the gangway. He was dressed in a magnificent cloak and with an equally magnificent feather cap on his head. The chanting died, a voice called out. It was suddenly clear that the king had come out only to escort Cook to the shore, where the ceremonies were to take place, and would not again be coming on board.

Cook was pulled ashore in his pinnace, King had already turned out the marines' guard, who made their usual dishevelled and sloppy showing. The formal meeting was to take place in Bayly's largest tent, and the lieutenant observed carefully the king and his entourage as they approached from the shore. Flanking the king were his sons, and following behind a number of chiefs; the king's nephew Chief Kamehameha, a ferocious-looking individual with his long hair plastered all over with paste and powder; a particularly vigorous and important looking Chief Kalimu; another muscular individual, Chief Ku'a, and several more. A parade as formidable as it was bizarre.

King watched Cook waiting patiently for the ceremonies to begin, a weary expression on his face, towering above all these islanders in spite of his middle-aged stoop. Then the king stepped forward, standing erect and without assistance but shaking all over as badly as High Priest Koa.

It was not until this moment, when in turn the king tore off his cloak and put it around Cook's shoulders, and then lifted his hat and placed it on Cook's head, that he exposed his face for the first time. Like the high priest's, it was peeling and covered in sores, the eyes were red and watery, but the expression through the ravages of kava was happy and benign.

To the lieutenant's astonishment, the King of Hawaii was none other than the Terreeoboo they had met off Maui: it was King Terreeoboo receiving the great god Lono himself.

Richard Hough

The Last Voyage of Captain James Cook

Captain James Cook Royal Navy, F.R.S. 1728-1779 by Nathaniel Dance

National Maritime Museum

Captain James LONO COOK

carefully 'DOCTORED' by

Ralph STEADman

SOUTH POINT

We had been trying to take his boat out for almost a week, but the sea was so rough that there was no point in even leaving the harbor. "We could probably get out," he said, "but we'd never get back in."

After a week of bad drinking and brooding, Captain Steve finally came up with a plan. If it was true that the weather was really turned around, then logic decreed that the normally savage waters on the *other* side of the island would now be calm as a lake.

"No problem," he assured me. "It's South Point for us, Big Guy. Let's get the boat ready. . . ."

Which we did. But the surf got worse, and after five or six more days of grim waiting, my brain began to go soft. We drove to the tops of volcanoes, we drank heavily, set off many bombs. . . . More storms came, the bills mounted up, and the days dragged by like dead animals.

As New Year's Eve approached it was clear that we were going to have to do something desperate to get in the water. In lieu of diving, fishing or even swimming, Juan and I had been forced to take up golf, a game I hadn't played in twenty years—not since the days when me and Bill Smith anchored the Male High School Golf Team back in Louisville and lost every match we played. We all have our winter dreams, and bad golf is one of mine . . . but it is not the kind of thing you want to have to resort to as a final retreat from the surf.

On the night before Juan was scheduled to fly back to his holding-pen in Colorado, we had a kind of final family send-off dinner for him at the Kona Inn. Captain Steve had called earlier that day to say that the swell was finally down enough so that we could probably risk getting out of the harbor tomorrow, but by this time nobody believed anything he said and the trip to South Point would need two days anyway . . . so even if it happened, we would have to do it alone.

Ralph was off the water completely and forever. His one trip on the boat had been such a nightmare that he had focused all his remaining energies to whatever could be found on the shore. His trip to the Volcano House had not yielded much, so now he was determined to confront both the ghost of Captain Cook and the legend of King Kamehameha at the same time. Ever since I'd told him that the official "Captain Cook Monument" on the wrong side of Kealakekua Bay was in fact a deeded piece of England on U.S. soil, he had made up his mind to go there and do whatever Englishmen do when they find some far corner of England to cling to on the edge of some foreign isle.

The access by sea was easy, but not in Kona weather; so he said he would take the whole family in by the land route, a tortuous five-mile hike down the cliffs from the highway. The walk *down* was not bad, but getting out was something else again. Anna and Sadie were ready to make the hike and worship at the only shrine they had.

It was a nasty trip, and I wanted no part of it. Captain Steve and I had seen it from his boat, the *Haere Marue*, on an earlier trip down the coast. The Cook monument was a small marble pillar like a miniature Washington Monument perched out on the edge of the black rocks. The U.S. government officially and formally *gave* this tiny piece of land to England, as a gesture of diplomatic gratitude for all that Captain Cook had done: he had given his life, in fact, to discover a pile of rocks in the middle of the Pacific that would later become the 50th state of the Union and our only real base in the Pacific.

The history of Hawaii is so fouled with greed, bungling, and dumb cowboy diplomacy, that the decadent gang ruling England at the time should have been hung by their heels like Mussolini for letting these islands go in exchange for a pillar of concrete. England might have controlled the whole Pacific for the next two hundred years, if the Earl of Sandwich hadn't been so deeply involved at the time with sponsoring King George III for membership in the Hellfire Club that he couldn't see anything beyond the end of his own gnarled organ. The Earl was into orgies that year, and the King was trying to cope with a nasty little insurrection called "The American Revolution." By the time Captain Cook hit the beach at Kealakekua Bay the British Army was mired down in Virginia at a place called Yorktown, the Earl of Sandwich—the first Lord of the Admiralty and the patron for whom these islands were originally named—was so busy running women in and out of the Hellfire Club that he barely had time to think about anything else.

Not even Sir Francis Dashwood, one of the most infamous degenerates ever to walk the streets of London or anywhere else, saw the need to take time out from his talks with Benjamin Franklin to consider the implications of the fact that his friend Sandwich had in fact discovered a place that might have allowed England to control the whole Pacific Ocean.

The first person I saw when we walked into the Kona Inn that night was Ackerman. He was sitting at the Kona Inn bar with a sleazy-looking person in bell-bottom Levi's whom I recognized as a notorious dope lawyer from California, a man

Kamehameha seems to have been early distinguished by enterprise, energy, decision of character, and unwearied perseverance in the accomplishment of his objects. Added to these, he possessed a vigorous constitution, and an unrivaled acquaintance with all the warlike games and athletic exercises of his country. To these qualities of mind and body he was probably indebted for the extensive power and protracted dominion which he exercised over the Sandwich Islands.

Kamehameha was undoubtedly a prince possessing shrewdness and great strength of character. During his reign, the knowledge of the people was much enlarged, and their comforts in some respects increased; their acquisition of iron tools facilitated many of their labors; the introduction of firearms changed their mode

of warfare; and in many cases, cloth of European manufacture was substituted for that made of native bark. But these improvements appear to be rather the result of their intercourse with foreigners, than of any measures of their sovereign; though the encouragement he gave to all foreigners visiting the islands was, no doubt, advantageous in these respects.

He has been called the Alfred of the Hawaiians; but he appears rather to have been their Alexander, ambition and a desire of conquest having been his ruling passions during the greater part of his life, though toward its close avarice superseded them.

The Journal of William Ellis

we'd met at one of the Marathon parties in Honolulu where he was passing out his business cards to everybody within reach and saying, "Hang on to this—you'll need me sooner or later."

Jesus, I thought. These leeching bastards are *everywhere*. First they only smoked the stuff, then they started selling it, and now they're gnawing at the roots of the whole drug culture like a gang of wild moles. They will be standing like pillars of salt at all our doorways when the great bell rings.

One of the reasons I'd come to Hawaii was to get away from lawyers for a while, so I herded our party in the other direction and down to our table looking out on the seawall.

Ralph and Anna and Sadie were already there, and Ralph was raving drunk. As we approached the table, he looked up at Captain Steve and snarled: "*You* again! What lies are you selling tonight? More fish stories?"

Steve smiled nervously. "No, Ralph. No lies tonight. I've learned my lesson—you're a bad man to lie to."

"Not like me," I said. "I'm easy. We're off to South Point tomorrow." I sat down at the table and lit a joint, which nobody seemed to notice. Ralph was staring at me with a look of shock and disgust on his face.

"I can't believe it," he muttered. "You're really going out on that silly boat again?"

I nodded. "That's right, Ralph. We finally figured it out—if this side of the island is rough, then the other side *must* be calm." Captain Steve smiled and shrugged his shoulders, as if the logic spoke for itself.

"And South Point," I continued, "is the closest place we can get to the other side, that's where the weather breaks."

"You should come with us, Ralph," said Captain Steve. "It'll be calm as a lake down there, and it's a real mysterious place."

"It's the land of Po," I said. "A desolate bottomless pit in the ocean, within sight of the cliffs on shore." I nodded wisely. "You've been looking for King Kam's burial place—maybe South Point is it."

Ralph gave me the stink-eye, but said nothing. He had already fallen in love with King Kamehameha—mainly on the basis of what little he knew about the "Law of the Splintered Oar" —and he was convinced that our story lay somewhere in the ancient burial caves around the City of Refuge and Kealakekua Bay. In any case, it was not at sea. "There *are* no fish," he muttered once again, "not even on the menu. All they have tonight is some kind of frozen mush from Taiwan."

"Don't worry, Ralph," I said. "We'll have all the fresh fish we can eat when I get back from South Point. Once we get around the corner down there to some calm waters I will plunder this sea like no man has ever plundered it before."

My fiancée was giving *me* the stink-eye now. Juan was staring up at the ceiling fan and Captain Steve was grinning like it all made good sense.

Just then I felt a hand on my shoulder. "Hello, Doc," said a voice behind me. "I've been wondering where you were."

I swung quickly around in my chair to see Ackerman smiling down at me, and the arm he extended was still blue. I stood up and we shook hands, then I introduced him around the table. Nobody really cared. We had already met too many strange people, by Ralph's count, and it was clear that Steve already knew him. Laila eyed his blue arm and gave a curt nod, as if some odd and disturbing scent had wafted through the room.

I was glad to see Ackerman, and now that he'd shaken the dope lawyer I stood up and took him aside. We walked out to the lawn and I handed him the joint. "Hey," I said. "How'd you like to make a run down to South Point tomorrow?"

"What?" he said. "South Point?"

"Yeah," I replied. "Just you and me and Steve. He says the weather should be okay, once we get around the point."

He laughed. "That's insane," he said, "but what the hell, why not? Steve's okay. He's a pretty good sailor."

"Good," I said, "let's do it. At least we'll get out on the water."

He chuckled. "Yeah. We *will* do *that.*" He finished off the joint and flipped it into the sea. "I'll bring some chemicals," he said. "We may need them."

"Chemicals?"

He nodded. "Yeah. I have some powerful organic mescaline. I'll bring it along."

"Right," I said. "That's a good idea— in case we get tired."

He slapped me on the back as we walked inside to the table. "Welcome to the Kona Coast, Doc. You're about to get what you came for."

WE'RE **ALL E**QUAL IN THE **O**CEAN

I took Juan to the airport the next morning for the flight to Honolulu. He'd had a good time, he said—especially with the bombs and the high-speed driving lessons—but he was not unhappy to be leaving. "There's too much tension," he said. "Everybody seems just about to go crazy. I couldn't stand living this way very long."

"You'll learn," I said. "You get used to it after a while."

"Or else you go nuts," he said with a grin. We were walking down the breezeway toward the Aloha Airlines loading gate, surrounded by dozens of Japs.

"Yeah," I said. "That's right. Totally nuts."

We walked the rest of the way in silence. The look on his face was pensive, vaguely amused. When we got to the gate the plane was about to leave, so he had to run for it. I watched him loping across the tarmac toward the plane and smiled. How long has he known—I thought—that Uncle Ralph is crazy?

On the way back to town I stopped by the *Haere Marue* and found Captain Steve already on the boat, wrestling tanks of compressed air off the dock and into a storage locker near the stern. He looked up as I scrambled down the ledge of black rocks to where the boat was tied up. "Ackerman was just here," he said. "I guess he's serious about making the trip."

"Yeah," I said. "I gave him the grocery list."

"I know," he said. "He's gone to Tanagughi's to get the stuff. All we need now is booze."

"And ice," I said, turning to climb back up the rocks. "How's the weather look?"

"No problem," he said, glancing out toward the sea. "The storm finally broke."

When I arrived at the Union Jack Liquor Store in the middle of downtown Kailua, Ackerman was waiting for me in a Datsun pickup full of grocery bags. "I got everything," he said. "You owe me three hundred and fifty-five dollars."

"Good God," I muttered. Then we went into the Union Jack and loaded up my VISA card with four cases of Heineken beer, two quarts each of Chivas Regal and Wild Turkey, two bottles of gin and a gallon of orange juice, along with six bottles of their best wines and another six bottles of champagne for the cocktail party that night.

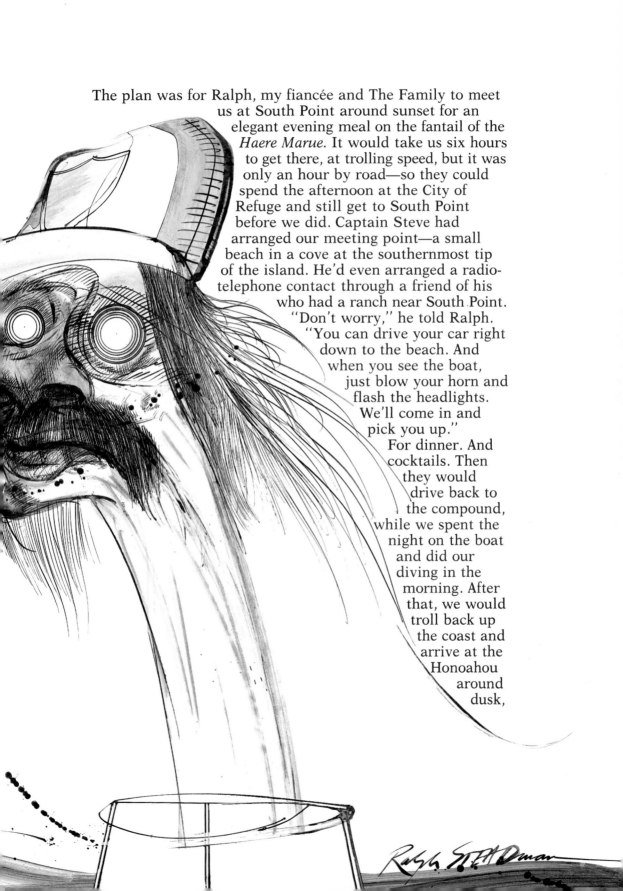

The plan was for Ralph, my fiancée and The Family to meet us at South Point around sunset for an elegant evening meal on the fantail of the *Haere Marue.* It would take us six hours to get there, at trolling speed, but it was only an hour by road—so they could spend the afternoon at the City of Refuge and still get to South Point before we did. Captain Steve had arranged our meeting point—a small beach in a cove at the southernmost tip of the island. He'd even arranged a radio-telephone contact through a friend of his who had a ranch near South Point. "Don't worry," he told Ralph. "You can drive your car right down to the beach. And when you see the boat, just blow your horn and flash the headlights. We'll come in and pick you up."

For dinner. And cocktails. Then they would drive back to the compound, while we spent the night on the boat and did our diving in the morning. After that, we would troll back up the coast and arrive at the Honoahou around dusk, for another cocktail party and a big fish dinner at home.

That was the plan. No problem at all. We would cruise down to South Point and have dinner on the fantail.

We left the Honokau not long after ten-thirty, poking carefully through a crust of smoking driftwood in the harbor. A boat had caught fire the night before and burned to the waterline. It was the *Blue Pacific*, Lee Marvin's old boat. There had been some kind of long dispute about ownership, Ackerman explained, and now the dispute was over.

"Jesus Christ," said Captain Steve as he eased his own boat through the dirty smoking debris. "They won't collect any insurance on that one. I can smell the kerosene from out here."

The two charter boats on either side of the *Blue Pacific* were being soaked down with hoses by potbellied Hawaiians aiming nozzles from the dock. They waved cheerfully as we idled out of the harbor. Captain Steve waved back and yelled something about the surf being up. The smoke in the harbor put a haze between us and the hot morning sun. As we passed the main channel buoy I looked back and saw the peaks of both *Mauna Lea* and *Mauna Koa* in the sky for the first time since I'd been there. The whole island is normally covered with a hamburger-shaped cloud for most of every day, but this morning of our departure for South Point was a rare exception.

I took it as a good omen, but I was wrong. By nightfall we would find ourselves locked in a death battle with the elements, wallowing helplessly in the worst surf I'd ever seen and half crazy with fear and strong chemicals.

We brought it on ourselves. No doubt about that. Ackerman knew it was crazy from the start—and so, I suspect, did Captain Steve. I was the one who'd fallen for this lunatic scheme: right, we'll just make a six-hour run down the coast, then duck around a corner to some rumor of a protected cove and dive in a forest of black coral. No problem. Invite the whole family down for dinner. We'll just go in and pick them up on the beach. . . .

We had both the *Wall Street Journal* and *Soldier of Fortune* on the boat. I had put them on my card at the Union Jack, but the run down to South Point was not calm enough for reading. We staggered around the boat like winos for most of the trip, keeping the boat headed due south against a crossing sea. The swell was coming strong out of the southwest. At one point we stopped to pick up a rotted life preserver with the words "Squire/Java" painted in the cork.

Captain Steve spent most of his time at the wheel high up on the flying bridge, while Ackerman and I stayed down in the cockpit smoking marijuana and waiting for the reels to go off.

I had long since got over the notion that just because we were

fishing we were going to catch fish. The whole idea of trailing
big-bore lines from the outriggers and rumbling along at trolling
speed was absurd. The only way we were going to get any fish,
I insisted, was by going over the side with scuba tanks and spear
guns, to hunt them where they lived. Every once in a while
either Ackerman or I would take a turn at the wheel, but never
for very long. Captain Steve was convinced that we might hook
a marlin or at least a big ahi at any moment, and he wanted to
be at the controls when it happened. He spent most of the
afternoon on the bridge, staring down at the barren, deep gray
water through polarized fishing glasses.

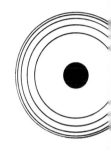

Ackerman seemed to share my aggressive pessimism about the
possibility of catching fish, but he kept a professional eye on
the lines anyway. "I *am* the first mate," he explained, "and I
have a certain professional pride." I had almost forgotten that
he was a part of that tight little tribe of licensed charter captains
that forms the only real elite on the Kona Coast. "We're all
equal in the ocean," he explained. "That's surfer talk, but it
makes a weird kind of sense."

I agreed. It was understood, in some way that has only to do
with the sea, that *either* of us would be capable of getting the
boat safely back into the harbor if Captain Steve, for some
reason, could not.

Ackerman was obviously at home on the boat. He knew where
everything went, and why, and not much was going to
surprise him. I'd invited him to come along without
giving it much thought, but only after hearing
Steve say several times that they were
"pretty close friends."

There *were* no fish. We trolled all the way down, but the only
signs of life we saw between Kailua and South Point was a school
of porpoises and some birds. It was a long hot ride, and by
mid-afternoon all three of us were jabbering drunk on beer.

It was just before sundown when we finally rounded the corner
at South Point. The sea had been rough on the run down the
Kona side of the island—but it was nothing compared to what
we encountered when we came around the point.

The sea was so high and wild that we could only gape at it.
No words were necessary. We had found our own hurricane,
and there was no place to hide from it.

At sundown I switched to gin and Ackerman broke out a small
vial of white powder that he sniffed up his nose off the tip of
a number 10 fish hook, then offered the vial to me.

"Be careful," he said. "It's not what you think."

I stared at the vial, examining the contents closely and
bracing my feet on the deck as the boat suddenly tilted and went
up on the hump of a swell.

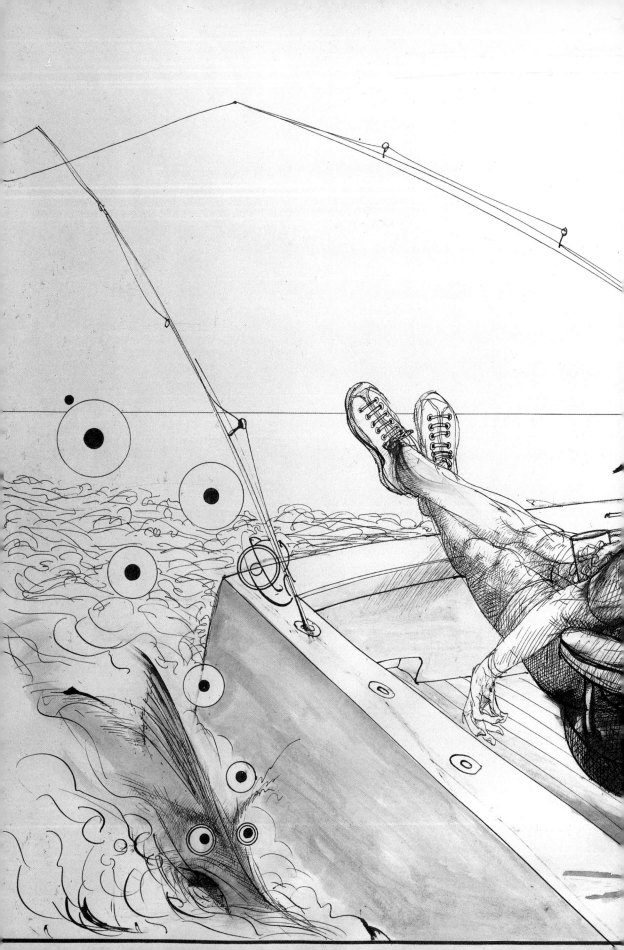

"It's China White," he said, gripping the back of the fighting chair as we came down hard in the slough.

Jesus, I thought. I'm out here with junkies. The boat rolled again, throwing me off balance on the wet deck with a cup of gin in one hand and a vial of heroin in the other.

I dropped them both as I slid past Ackerman and grabbed the ladder to keep from going over the side.

Ackerman lunged for the vial with the speed of a young cobra and caught it on one bounce, but it was already wet and he stared at it balefully, then tossed it away in the sea. "What the hell," he said. "I never liked the stuff anyway."

I pulled myself over to the chair and sat down. "Me either," I said. "It's hard on the stomach."

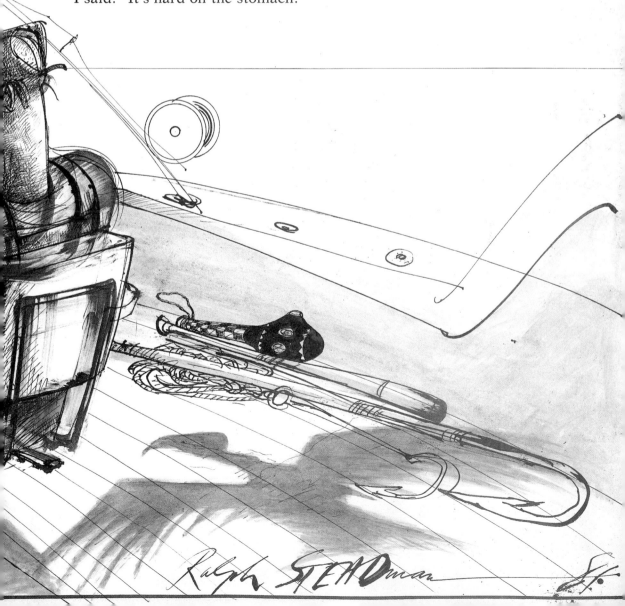

Ralph STEADman

He eyed me darkly for a moment and I planted both feet, not knowing what to expect. It is bad business to drop other people's heroin—especially far out at sea with a storm coming up—and I didn't know Ackerman that well. He was a big rangy bastard, with the long loose muscles of a swimmer, and his move on the bouncing vial had been impressively fast. I knew he could get me with the gaffing hook before I reached the ladder.

I resisted the urge to call Captain Steve. Were they *both* junkies? I wondered, still poised on the edge of the white naugahyde chair. What kind of anglers carry China White to work?

"It's a good drug for the ocean," Ackerman said, as if I'd been thinking out loud. "A lot of times it's the only way to keep from killing the clients."

I nodded, pondering the long night ahead. If the first mate routinely snorted smack at the cocktail hour, what was the captain into?

It occurred to me that I didn't really know either one of these people. They were strangers, and now I was trapped on a boat with them, twenty miles off the far western edge of America with the sun going down and deep black water all around us.

The land was out of sight now, lost in a desolate night fog. The sun went down and the *Haere Marue* rumbled on through the waves toward South Point, the terrible Land of Po. The red and green running lights on our bow were barely visible from the stern, barely thirty feet away. The night closed around us like smoke, cold and thick with the smell of our diesel exhaust fumes.

It was almost seven o'clock when the last red glow of the sun disappeared, leaving us to run blind and alone by the compass. We sat for a while on the stern, listening to the sea and the engines and the occasional dim crackling of voices on the shortwave radio up above the high-bridge, where Captain Steve was perched, like some kind of ancient mariner.

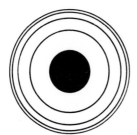
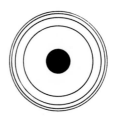
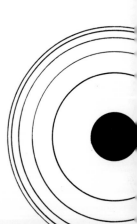

THE LAND OF PO

The sea was not getting any calmer as we approached our destination, a small beach at the foot of sheer black cliffs. Captain Steve took us in about halfway, then slowed to a crawl and came scrambling down the ladder. "I don't know about this," he said nervously. "The swell seems to be picking up."

Ackerman was staring at the beach, where huge breakers foamed.

The first alarm came from Captain Steve, up above, when he suddenly shut down the engines and came back down the ladder.

"Get ready," he said. "We're in for a long night." He stared nervously into the sea for a moment, then darted into the cabin and began hauling out life jackets.

"Forget it," said Ackerman. "Nothing can save us now. We may as well eat the mescaline." He cursed Captain Steve again. "This is your fault, you stupid little bastard. We'll all be dead before morning."

Captain Steve shrugged as he swallowed the pill. I ate mine and set about assembling the hibachi I'd bought that morning to cook our fresh fish dinner. Ackerman leaned back in his chair and opened a bottle of gin.

We spent the rest of the night raving at each other and wandering distractedly around the boat like rats cast adrift in a shoebox, scrambling around the edges and trying to keep away from each other. The casual teamwork of the sundown hours became a feverish division of labor, with each of us jealously tending our own sector.

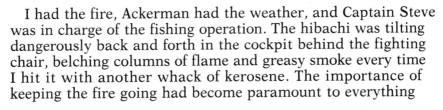

I had the fire, Ackerman had the weather, and Captain Steve was in charge of the fishing operation. The hibachi was tilting dangerously back and forth in the cockpit behind the fighting chair, belching columns of flame and greasy smoke every time I hit it with another whack of kerosene. The importance of keeping the fire going had become paramount to everything

else, despite the obvious and clearly suicidal danger.
We had three hundred gallons of diesel fuel in
the tanks down below, and any queer pitch
of sea could have spilled flaming charcoal
all over the cockpit and turned the
whole boat into a fireball—
putting all three of us in the water,
where we would be instantly
picked up in the surf and dashed
to death on the rocks.

No matter, I thought. We *must*
keep the fire going. It had become
a symbol of life, and I was not about to
let it die down.

The others agreed. We had long since
abandoned any idea of cooking anything
for dinner—and in fact we had thrown most
of the food overboard by that time,
thinking to use it for bait—but we
all understood that as long as
the fire burned, we *would*
survive. My appetite had
died around sundown,
and now I was covered
with layers of cold mescaline sweat.
Every once in a while a shudder
would race up my spine, causing my
whole body to tremble. In these moments
my conversation would suddenly collapse,
without warning, and my voice would quaver
hysterically for a few seconds while I
tried to calm down.

"Jesus," I said to Captain Steve some time around midnight, "it's lucky you got rid of that cocaine. The last thing we need right now is some kind of crank."

He nodded wisely, still watching the flashlight in the water, then suddenly spun around in the chair and uttered a series of wild cries. His eyes were unnaturally bright and his lips seemed to flap as he spoke. "Oh yes!" he blurted. "Oh hell yes. That's the *last* thing we need!"

I backed away from him, not taking my eyes off his hands. Ackerman was nowhere in sight, but I could hear the staccato bleating of his voice from what seemed like a hundred miles away. He was up on the bow, pacing around with a gaffing hook in his hands, watching for shifts in the wind and screaming at the lights on the faraway cliff.

"You brainless Jap bastards!" he yelled. "Douse those goddamn lights!"

Captain Steve was now leaning over the back of the boat sinking another hot dog down on the end of our line with the flashlight. "What the hell is wrong with those Japs?" he muttered. "Are they trying to signal us in?"

"Yeah," I said. "It's an old Key West trick—set up a false lighthouse and lure boats onto the rocks."

Suddenly he leaped back and shouted, "Oh my God, a sea snake!"

"What?"

"A sea snake!" he said, pointing down at the water. "Lethal poison, instant death! It came right up to my hand!"

I shrugged, firing another stream of kerosene into the hibachi and sending another balloon of yellow fire up into the night. I grabbed the bucket of water that I was keeping on the deck for emergencies. Captain Steve staggered sideways, shielding his face from the flames. "Be careful!" he shouted. "Leave that fire alone!"

"Don't worry," I said, "I know what I'm doing."

His hands were clawing nervously at his pockets. "Where is it?" he hissed. "Did I give you the bottle?"

"What bottle?"

He fell sideways and grabbed the chair as another big wave picked us up. "The *kind!*" he screamed. "Who has the goddamn *kind?*"

I was hanging on to one tin leg of the hibachi, which had almost turned over. Finally, the wave passed and we settled back into the slough. "You fool," I said, "it's gone. You took it over the side."

"What are you talking about?" he screamed. *"What side?"*

I watched his eyes for a moment, then shook my head and

went back into the cabin for a beer. Captain Steve had never tried mescaline before, and I could see that it was reaching his brain. It was obvious from the confusion in his eyes that he had no recollection at all of taking our last bottle of stimulant down with him, in the pocket of his trunks, when he'd gone down with the scuba tanks to secure our anchor line around a big rock on the bottom, about 90 feet down. I had grabbed the bottle away from him when he came up and drunk about half of the salty bitter mixture in one swallow. Ackerman, quickly understanding the nature of the tragedy, had drunk off the rest.

We had no choice. There is no point trying to save cocaine after you've mixed it up with salt water. Captain Steve had missed his share—which was fair, I thought, and probably just as well. Any fool who will dive to the bottom of the Pacific Ocean with two grams of cocaine in his pocket is capable of anything at all; and now he was losing his grip to the psychedelics.

Bad business, I thought. It's time to collect the knives.

I woke up at sunrise to find Ackerman passed out like a dead animal from an overdose of Dramamine and Captain Steve wandering frantically around the cockpit, grappling with a tangle of ropes and saying over and over to himself, "Holy Jesus, man! Let's get out of here!"

I came awake and stumbled up from the cabin where I'd spent two hours sleeping on a cushion covered with fishhooks. We were still in the shadow of the cliffs and the morning wind was cold. The fire had gone out and our thermos bottle of coffee had cracked open sometime during the night. The deck was awash with a slimy mixture of kerosene and floating soot.

But the wind had not shifted. Captain Steve had been awake all night, he explained, never taking his eyes off the anchor line and ready, at any moment, to leap into the surf and swim for it.

"I'll never understand how we survived," he muttered, staring up at the cliffs where the colony of mean Japs was still clustered around their campfires. "Now I know what they mean about South Point. It *is* a dangerous place."

"The Land of Po," I said.

"Yeah," he said, reeling in the last of our all-night fishing lines. All the hot dogs had been gnawed off by eels, but the hooks were otherwise clean. Not even a sea snake had taken our wrong-minded bait, and the water all around us was littered with floating debris: beer bottles, orange peels, plastic baggies and mangled tuna fish cans. About ten yards off the stern was an empty Wild Turkey bottle with a piece of paper inside.

Ackerman had tossed it over some time during the night, after finishing off the whiskey and stuffing the bottle with a sheet of Kona Inn stationery on which I had scrawled: "Beware. There ARE no fish." I thought it would be halfway to Guam by now, a warning to other fools who might try to fish in the Land of Po.

Captain Steve was staring glumly over the side of the boat at the anchor line. "All we have to do now," he said, "is haul up the anchor and get the hell out of this place." He shook his head and made a nervous whistling noise. "Let me tell you one thing for sure," he added, "we are *lucky to be alive* right now. That's the worst night I ever spent in my life." He pointed in the general direction of land, where the surf was still pounding and foaming against the rocks. "One shift in the wind," he said, "could have swung us around so fast that I couldn't even have got the engine started. We'd be driftwood by now."

He was still staring down at the anchor line. The other end of it, I knew, was tied securely around a rock far below, and we both understood what would have to be done. There was no way to haul it up, or to maneuver it loose with the boat. We would have to either chop the line and leave the anchor behind, or somebody would have to go down with a tank and untie the knot.

We stood there for a while on the fantail, staring down at the cold black water. Ackerman was out of the question, so it was either me or Captain Steve. He had gone down the night before, and I knew it was my turn now. That was fair. That was the rule of the sea, a true cornerstone of the macho way of life.

I zipped up my jacket and opened a beer. "How much do anchors cost?" I asked him.

He shrugged. "Well . . . with ninety feet of line, at, say, about two dollars a foot. . . ." He seemed to be adding it up very carefully in his mind.

"Yeah," he said finally. "Call it four hundred, maybe four fifty."

"That's cheap," I said, reaching for my belt knife. "I'll give you a check." I leaned out to grab the anchor line with my other hand, preparing to cut us loose. Nothing short of extreme physical violence could have got me in the water that morning.

Captain Steve stayed my hand before I could slash the line. "Wait a minute," he said. "I can't go back to the harbor with no anchor. They'd laugh me out of town."

"Fuck those people," I said. "They weren't on the boat last night."

He was strapping on the tanks.

I watched him go over the side and disappear.

It was 4 February, a fine, warm early morning. The natives of Kealakekua Bay were up early for the word had got about that the great ships were leaving. The shores on both sides, divided by that great black slab of cliff, were thick with dark bodies, some waving white cloths.

For Cook's men there was a strong measure of regret at parting after the contentment occasioned by this visit. For the Hawaiians, it had been a strange two and a half weeks, busy, emotional, traumatic even, like no other period in their lives or their history: an unpredicted divine descent upon the steady round of the seasons; an event of great satisfaction paid for at a great price.

By the early morning of 6 February they were at the northern extremity of a deep bay just south of the northern tip of Hawaii, Upolu Point. They had all but completed their clockwise circumnavigation of the island, in accordance with the legendary annual practice of Lono. Then it came on to blow very hard for 36 hours.

On 8 February, three years to the day—almost to the hour—since Cook had volunteered at the Admiralty to command this voyage, the *Resolution*'s foremast split.... They could not proceed in this condition, especially as the old leak under the buttock had opened up again like an unhealable wound.

In the storm-swept dawn light, Cook had to make the critical decision on where to put in for repairs. Should he continue to Maui and trust that he would find shelter on the west or southerly coast, which he had not yet traced? Or perhaps to another island? Kauai and Niihau had already proved unpromising. In all their sailing among these islands, Kealakekua Bay was the only safe anchorage they had discovered.

To give himself time, Cook sent Bligh across the storm-tossed waters to acquaint Clerke of their situation. Now both ships' companies were conscious of their dilemma. They had already been too long at Kealakekua Bay. They had cleared the whole area of its immediately available food. All those hogs could not have been given to them without depriving the people of supplies. Repairs would take at least a week, probably two weeks.

Cook set himself upon the safer of the two courses open to him, and at 10 a.m. on the morning of 8 February, the two sloops bore away south for their old anchorage, "all hands much chagrined," wrote King, "and damning the foremast."

Richard Hough

The Last Voyage of Captain James Cook

Ackerman woke up while Captain Steve was down and I told him the story. "That crazy bastard," he muttered, reaching down for a diving knife that he kept in a sheath around his leg. "Start the engine. Let him *swim* back." He began to cut the line, then hesitated and pulled back. "No," he said, "the minute we start the engine, he'll hear the noise and come up like a rocket. We'll have a case of the bends on our hands."

Captain Steve finally emerged from the depths and signaled me to haul in the anchor. Twenty minutes later we were out of the surf and running north at easy trolling speed. The Captain had gone groggy while we were hauling him back into the boat and dropped his scuba tank on Ackerman's foot, crushing his big toe and putting blood all over the deck. Ackerman gobbled another handful of Dramamine and fell into a deep stupor. We put his foot in an ice bag and stretched him out like a corpse on a cushion in the shade of the bridge.

I took the helm while Captain Steve set the outriggers. "Are you out of your goddamn mind?" I yelled down at him from my perch on the tuna tower. "Get away from those lines! Go to sleep."

"No!" he shouted. "This is a *fishing* boat! We *must* catch fish."

The strain of the long night at South Point was beginning to tell on him. His eyes had swollen up like rotten eggs and he had chewed his own lips so severely during the night that now he could barely talk. When he tried to climb back to the bridge he lost his grip on the ladder and fell on his back in the cockpit, where he thrashed wildly around on the deck in a puddle of bloody filth.

It was an ugly thing to see. From my seat on the bridge I could look straight down on the main deck of the *Haere Marue* and see both the captain and the first mate badly disabled. One appeared to be dead, with his mouth hung open and his eyes rolled back in his head, and the other was twitching around like a fish with a broken neck.

The maze of human wreckage down below looked like something King Kam might have brought back to Kona in one of his war canoes that got caught in an ambush on Maui. We were victims of the same flaky hubris that had killed off the cream of Hawaiian warriors in the time of the Great Wars. We had gone off in a frenzy of conquest—to the wrong place at the wrong time and probably for all the wrong reasons—and now we were limping back home with our decks full of blood and our nerves turned to jelly. All we could hope for, now, was no more trouble and a welcoming party of good friends and beautiful women at the dock. After that, we could rest and lick our wounds.

I couldn't leave the wheel, or the boat would start running

in circles and tangle its own propeller in the long fishing lines
we were trailing. In order to keep the lures on the surface I
had to maintain a constant engine speed of 1750rpm and keep
moving straight ahead. Any variation in either the speed or
the course might be ruinous. If we fouled the prop and lost power
it would mean calling for help on the radio, then wallowing
helplessly around in the waves for eight hours until a rescue
boat arrived to tow us in.

That was unacceptable. The crew was in no condition to
endure another day and night at sea. I aimed the boat closer
to shore and put a bit of weight on the throttle. If a straight
line is the shortest distance between two points, I reasoned,
then a straight line at top speed would be even shorter.

I was still congratulating myself on my breakthrough into
higher mathematics when I was startled by a squawk from
below. I looked over the rail to see Captain Steve on his knees
in the stern, pointing frantically back at his carefully set lures—
which were now almost airborne, bouncing across the water
like flying fish. "Slow it down!" he was screaming. "Are you
crazy?"

Crazy? I thought. I almost hurled a beer bottle down on his
neck. The course he had set would have taken us far out to
sea through the marlin grounds, a lazy parabolic loop that would
have added another two or three hours to the trip. He was still
obsessed with the notion that we were going to catch fish. I
could see it in his eyes, the feverish gleam of Ahab.

"Forget it," I yelled down to him. "The joke's over. It's time
to go home."

The anguished look on his face told me it was useless to argue
with him. There was no room in his mind for the idea of
coming back to port without a fish; and I had a feeling he might
go over the side at any moment with a knife in his teeth, if
that's what it took to get one.

And it was, after all, *his* boat. I was not ready for mutiny,
so I eased off on the throttle and altered our course. This seemed
to satisfy him. He went back to fussing with the lines and
drinking beer. I settled back in the catbird seat and listened to
the radio for a while, feeling drowsy as the sun got hotter and
hotter. Every once in a while some outburst of gibberish on the
radio would wake me up:

"... calling *Humdinger*, do you read me?"

Long pause and crackling of static, then:

"Goddammit, goddammit, yes, goddammit, yes, this is
Humdinger. I read you, what's your location? Over."

"The wrong place, over."

(Harsh laughter and more crackling static . . .)

"Well goddammit you stay there, you bastard, don't come anywhere near me."

"What? Say that again, *Humdinger.*"

"Stay away! I got two nekkid women on board."

(Pause and crackling.)

"What's your location, *Humdinger*? I'm nekkid myself. Let's get together."

The banter went on for a while, then I lashed the wheel so the boat wouldn't wander and went down the ladder for a beer. Captain Steve had crawled into the cabin and passed out on top of the ice locker. I watched him for a while, making sure he was really sleeping, then I walked back to the stern and reeled in all the lines. Ackerman still looked dead and he seemed to be barely breathing, so I rolled him over on his side and hung a bell around his neck so I could hear him if he started vomiting.

Then I went back up on the bridge and aimed the boat straight for the harbor, taking it so close into shore that I could almost read the signs up on Highway One. I turned up the radio to cover the engine noise, then slowly increased our speed until we were planing across the waves like some kind of mongrel Cigarette boat. Ah ha, I thought, now *this* is the way to fish—just run the bastards down, chop their brains off with the prop and then circle back to pick up whatever's left.

Three hours later I stopped by the buoy outside the harbor and reeled out the fishing lines, then I twisted Ackerman's leg until he came thrashing awake like an alligator caught in a trap.

"Time to work," I said. "We're home."

He sat up and looked around, then slowly stood up and reached for the bottle of rum in the tool box.

"Where's the Captain?" he asked.

I pointed to Steve, still asleep on the ice locker, only inches from the rail. Ackerman walked over to him and put a foot in the small of his back, and shoved him violently over the side.

Captain Steve grabbed wildly for a hand-hold, then disappeared into the sea. He came sputtering to the surface, still not completely awake, and clawing desperately at the slippery side of the boat.

Ackerman wanted to drag him in with a gaffing hook, but I restrained him.

After we hauled Captain Steve back aboard he sulked for a while in the cockpit, then climbed up to take the wheel. He eased the boat into the harbor, squatting darkly in his seat on the bridge and avoiding the eyes of the smiling Kanakas on the gasoline dock.

Nobody was there to meet us, but it didn't matter. We were warriors, returned from the Land of Po, and we had terrible stories to tell. But not in the harbor, or at the bar in the Kona Inn. Our tale was too grim.

Captain Steve was still hunkered down on the bridge when Ackerman and I finished off-loading our gear and prepared to leave. "Where're you guys going?" he called out. "To Huggo's?"

I shrugged, too weak and whipped to care where I was going, just as long as it was away from the sea. I felt like driving up the mountain to Waimea and applying for a job as a cowboy on the Parker Ranch. Get back to the land for a while, drink gin all night and run around naked with the menehunes.

But when I mentioned this to Ackerman he shook his head. "No," he said. "There's only one place for us now—the City of Refuge."

THE BALCONY LIFE

It was time to leave. Ackerman's notion of fleeing to the City of Refuge had seemed like a good idea at the time, but the scene we found back at the compound on our return from South Point was too ugly to cure by anything as simple as a drive down the coast to some temple of ancient superstition where we may or may not have found refuge. Right, I thought, never mind that silly native bullshit. Where's a telephone? What we need now is a quick call to Aloha Airlines.

Ackerman agreed. We were both stunned by the chaos we saw when we turned the little VW convertible into the driveway. The same storm that had almost whipped us to death in the ocean off South Point the night before had moved north and was now pounding the Kona Coast with fifteen-foot waves and a blinding monsoon rain. On the way in from the Honokohau we'd seen cars and mopeds abandoned all along Alii Drive, which was littered with driftwood and jagged black rocks. Huge waves were breaking over the highway at Disappearing Beach—which

Everyone noticed the profound change in the atmosphere in the bay, and the contrast with their first arrival. The waters were empty of canoes, the black lowering line of cliff revealed not a single spectator along its crest. Some of Cook's men were uneasy, others, as King observed, felt their vanity hurt that they were so disregarded. Just as they were concluding that the entire population had been evacuated or struck down by some plague, a single canoe put off and headed for the *Discovery*. Up the sloop's gangway there climbed a ferocious looking chief wearing a fine red-feathered cloak. He was the king's nephew, Kamehameha, whose appearance had so alarmed them three weeks earlier when he had introduced himself with Terreeoboo's two sons. . . .

The sailmakers, carpenters and the marines, with King again in command, found no objection to their reinstalling themselves in the old field with their tents by the *heiau*. Bayly even got his clock and telescopes ashore with his tents. The priests seemed as friendly as before, and were ready to taboo the area again, and the carpenters were able to go about their special craft of cleaning out the mast's heel, dealing with the sprung fishes, shaping had long since disappeared, once again—and it took us almost two hours to get from the boat to the compound which was taking a serious surf.

Both houses were empty, the pool was swamped, the surf was foaming up on the porch and deck chairs were scattered around the lawn in a maze of what looked like red seaweed. On closer examination it turned out to be the slimy wet remnants of two or three hundred thousand Chinese firecrackers, a flood of red rice paper from the dozens of Chinese Thunder-bombs we'd been amusing ourselves with. I thought it had been washed out to sea—which was true, for a while—but it had not washed out far enough, and now the sea was tossing it back.

Ralph and The Family were gone. The door to their house stood open, and the place where he'd parked his car was ankle-deep in salt water. The fronts of both houses were gummed up with a layer of red slime and there was no sign of life anywhere. Everything was gone; both houses had been abandoned to the ravaging surf, and my first thought was that everything in them including the occupants had been sucked out to sea by riptides and bashed to death on the rocks.

Ackerman disagreed, saying they had all probably taken to

new ones from some hard toa wood they had providentially kept from Moorea.

On the following morning King Terreeoboo arrived in the bay as he had before, in great style and at a fine pace. At once the waters of the bay were un-tabooed, and suddenly it was almost as if nothing had changed since those days when there were always numberless canoes plying between shore and ships, and the noise and bustle of trading lasted from dawn to dusk.

But things were not the same. Just below the surface, violence now lurked among these Hawaiians. A great black seam of hostility had been thrust up close to the surface as if Mauna Loa's volcano had erupted again and a lava stream of hatred were about to flow.

King Terreeoboo, shaking and held steady by his two sons, came out to the *Resolution*. Why had they returned? What were they doing? How long this time? "He appeared much dissatisfied," noted Jem Burney.

Richard Hough

The Last Voyage of Captain James Cook

higher ground long before the surf began hitting the porches. That was standard procedure on Alii Drive in winter storms: first sirens, then roadblocks and panic, and finally forced evacuation of all beachfront homes by Civil Defense rescue teams. "It happens every year," he said. "We lose a few houses, a few cars, but not many people."

I was still rummaging through the bedrooms, looking for signs of life with one eye and watching the sea with the other. A big one, I knew, could come at any time with no warning at all, rolling over us like a bomb. I had a vision of Ralph clinging, even now, to some jagged black rock far out in the roaring white surf, screaming for help and feeling the terrible jaws of a wolf eel gripping his leg.

What would we do if we suddenly heard his screams and saw him thrashing around in the sea a hundred yards away?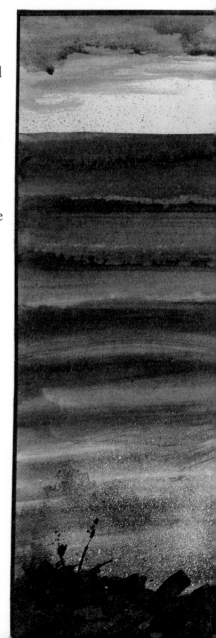

Nothing. We could only watch, as the waves tossed him up on the rocks, time after time. By morning he would be ripped to shreds.

I was tempted, for a moment, to get a big spotlight and look for him out there in the sea, but I didn't want to do it. What if I spotted him? The sight would haunt me for the rest of my life . . . I would have to watch him die, fixed in the beam of my own spotlight until he finally disappeared, wild eyes gleaming in the foam of a crashing wave, then sinking out of sight. . . .

I heard Ackerman's voice just as a monster wave hit the pool and blasted ten thousand gallons of water straight up in the air.

I scrambled over the porch railing and ran for the driveway. High ground, I thought. Uphill. Get out of here.

Ackerman was calling from the balcony of the caretaker's cottage. I rushed up the stairs, soaking wet, and found him sitting at a table with five or six people who were calmly drinking whiskey and smoking marijuana. All my luggage, including the typewriter, was piled in a corner of the porch.

Nobody had drowned, nobody was missing. I accepted a joint from my fiancée and breathed deeply. Ralph had flipped out sometime around noon, they explained, when the sea hurled a fifty-pound stalk of green bananas up on his porch, followed by a wave of red slime. Hundreds of dead fish washed up on the lawn, the house was suddenly filled with thousands of flying cockroaches, and the sea rolled under the floor.

The caretaker said Ralph had taken his family to the King Kamehameha Hotel on the pier in downtown Kailua, after failing to find seats on a night flight back to England. "Where's the dog?" I asked. I knew Sadie had become strongly attached

to the beast, and there was no sign of its corpse in the general wreckage of the compound.

"They took it with them," he said. "He asked me to give you this note." He handed me a crumpled piece of hotel stationery, damp and dark with Ralph's scrawl.

"I can't stand it anymore," it said. "The storm almost killed us. Don't call. Leave us alone. The hotel doctor will take care of Rupert and send him home after quarantine. Please make all arrangements. Do it for Sadie. Her hair is turning white. It was a terrible experience. I'll get even. Love, Ralph."

"Jesus," I said. "Ralph's gone. He went soft on us."

"He knew you'd say that," said the caretaker, accepting the joint from Ackerman and inhaling deeply. "That's why he left you the dog. He said it was the right thing to do."

I refolded the note and put it in my pocket. "Of course," I said. "Ralph is an artist. He has a very keen sense of right and wrong."

We sat on the porch for a while, smoking fresh marijuana and listening to the Amazing Rhythm Aces, then we drove up to Ackerman's for the night. The compound was flooded and water had soaked all the floors. There was no point in trying to sleep there.

Ralph was gone and I was too tired to call him on the phone. Soon the whole family would be on a plane back to England, clinging desperately to each other and too exhausted to sleep for more than two or three or four minutes at a time—like survivors of some terrible shipwreck, only half understanding what had happened to them, disturbing the other passengers with sporadic moans and cries, finally sedated by the stewardess.

Life is slow on the Kona Coast these days. The fish still feed and the sun still shines and the wind still blows up from Tahiti. . . . But there is a new kind of stillness in the air, which has nothing to do with the weather. Bad angst is rampant. People are jumping ship. The whole coast is for sale, and even the wild and beautiful Chang sisters are talking about a move to the mainland. The Kona Boom has gone bust, for a while, and the skimmers are pulling out.

Nothing I say will change their minds. People like me here, but they are reluctant to trust my judgment.

So I spend my nights on the balcony of 505, the Queen Kalama Suite in the King Kamehameha Hotel, which has a view of everything—the whole Kona waterfront, two snowcapped volcanos, and especially the municipal pier on Kailua Bay, where the action never stops.

I like it up here. I am cultivating a taste for the balcony life. The bill is still in Ralph's name, but no matter. The management will cover it. They have made themselves legally responsible for all problems involving Ralph's dog, which is still under international quarantine. It went mad in the kennel from fleas while under the personal supervision of the hotel veterinarian, and now they are legally responsible. Not only for Rupert but also for any brain damage, swelling, blindness, missed deadlines, loss of income and any other grief, pain or mental anguish resulting from my being stung in the eye by a wasp at the poolside bar. The creature flew into my face and got trapped behind my sunglasses, then it stung me three times in the eye socket. My head swelled up dangerously and all they gave me to cure it was a filthy sock full of ice, which hurt far worse than the sting. And when I asked for help they referred me to Doctor Ho, a "large animal" vet.

In any case, they have me on their hands now. I control the high ground, as it were, and I refuse to check out until we reach a settlement.

I have hired a Korean lawyer from Honolulu to negotiate my claim, which is huge . . . and in the meantime I have learned to enjoy this hotel, which is not a bad place to live. There are many fine shops downstairs, and three bars. There is also a big blue pool down below to my right, the Hulihee Palace on the waterfront to my left across the bay, and thick green lawns running out along the seawall to the House of Lono and the funeral site of Kamehameha the Great.

He died down there in a thatch-roof hut under the royal palm trees on the eighth day of May, 1819, at the age of 61. His body was burned in a firepit and his bones were buried in a secret cave by his main kahunas, who never disclosed the site. King Kam has many monuments in Hawaii, but no tombstone. The same kahunas who buried his bones also ate his heart, for the power that was in it—just as Kamehameha himself once fed on the heart of Captain Cook.

Stone Battle Axe

113

KICKING ASS IN KONA

At the end of the Kailua Municipal Pier is a huge set of scales, maintained by the Japs from the local icehouse who routinely buy every fish brought into the harbor and send it off to Tokyo, to be chopped up into *sushimi*, then refrozen and sent back to Los Angeles. Sushimi is big business all over the Pacific, and Japanese fish brokers control most of it.

A license to run sushimi out of Hawaii is better than having a slot machine concession in the Las Vegas airport. There is always more demand for sushimi than the market-fisherman can supply. The only thing that varies is the price—which ranges from five and sometimes ten dollars a pound at Christmas, down to twenty cents a pound at the peak of the sport-fishing season, which runs from May to September on the Kona Coast and yields between five and ten thousand pounds of sushimi for the market every day.

Ahi, the big yellowfin tuna, is not a real crowd-pleaser on the pier; but it sells for a lot more money. Ahi is *sushimi*—in LA and New York, as well as Tokyo—and in the weeks before Christmas when demand is running high, the dockside price for a big ahi in Kona can run up to five and sometimes ten dollars a pound.

Usually it is down around a dollar, which makes it a nice fish to come in with. But ahi is not the glamorous fish in Kona. This place is famous for marlin. *Big* marlin. And that's what the crowd on the pier wants to see. Any boat flying the traditional dark blue marlin flag on its fantail will change the mood of the crowd very suddenly.

The Kona Coast is the fishing capital of Hawaii, Kailua Bay is the social and commercial axis of the Kona Coast; and the huge gallows-like rig of fish-weight scales on the pier in front of the King Kam Hotel is where the fishing pros of Kona live or die every afternoon of the week—in full view of the public, such as it is.

Sport fishing is big business in Kona, and four o'clock on any afternoon at the end of the city pier is showtime for the local charter captains. That is where they bring their fish in to be weighed, and to have their pictures taken if they're bringing in anything big. The big scales at the end of the pier are where the victors show their stuff, and the vanquished don't even show up. The boats with no blood on their decks don't even come in to the pier; they take the short way home—to the harbor, eight miles north, and those last few miles in from the buoy can be a long and surly ride for a skipper with a boatload of clients who paid $500 a day to catch nothing at all. The Honokohau at sundown is not a happy place to be. As each boatload of failures ties up, the harbor curs rush to the edge of the black lava cliff that looks down on the dock and start barking. They want the leftover lunch meat, not fish, and it is an ugly scene to confront at the end of a long day of failure at sea.

On any given day most boats will go back to the Honokohau. But the few return to the pier, where the scene is entirely different—especially on a "hot day," when half the town has already been alerted by triumphant radio calls from far out at sea to prepare the scales for serious action when the fleet comes in.

The crowd will begin gathering on the end of the pier around three. Jimmy Sloan, the commercial photographer who has the pier concession, will be there with his camera to make the moment live in history on 8 × 10 glossies at $10 each. And there will also be the man from Grey's taxidermy, just in case you want your trophy mounted.

And if you don't, the little blue Datsun pickup from the Jap icehouse is there to haul it off for cash. Marlin goes cheap: twenty-five cents a pound, because only the Japs will eat it and the main market is in Tokyo, over three thousand miles away.

The boys who run the scales almost always know what is coming in, but they don't know when . . . which makes them act nervous, as four o'clock rolls around. Any skipper who has already reported a big fish on board will be in by dark, which doesn't leave much time.

The crowd knows this too. Rumors spread and tourists begin loading cameras. The boats will come in from the west, directly out of the sunset. On a calm day in summer you can stand on the end of the pier and see a boat coming from ten miles out at sea. At first it is just a white spot on the horizon. . . . Then a small glint of sunlight, reflected off the highest point of the steel tuna tower. . . . And soon the white spot of a roostertail of white spray churned up in the wake of a fast-approaching hull.

Soon the boat is close enough for people with good binoculars to see the color of the flag the boat is flying on the outrigger pole. The blue stands out better against a background of reddening Pacific sky than the white flag of the ahi—and it will get the crowd moving toward the scales a lot faster, when the first cry of "blue" goes up.

Every successful charter boat captain understands the difference between the Fishing Business and Show Business. Fishing is what happens out there on the deep blue water, and the other is getting strangers to pay for it. So when you come swooping into Kailua Bay at sunset with a big fish to hang up on the scales, you want to do it slowly. Ease into the bay in a long graceful arc, against a background of sailboats and volcanos, then back your boat down on the pier with every ounce of style and slow-rumbling boat-handling drama that you and your crew can muster.

The skipper is up on the flying bridge, facing the crowd and controlling the boat with both hands behind his back on the wheel and throttle. His deckhand and the clients will be standing down below on the stern, also facing the crowd and trying not to do anything wrong or awkward in these last crucial moments, as the boat backs slowly up to the scales and the chain-hoist swings out to pick up their fish.

Most of the "anglers" who have paid for the privilege of fishing for the big ones with the big boys in the world-record waters off Kona don't give a hoot in hell what happens to whatever fish they've caught, once they've had their pictures taken standing next to the beast as it hangs by its tail from the steel gallows on the end of the pier. The Bringing in of the Fish is the only action in town at that hour of the day—or any other hour, for that matter; because big-time fishing is what the Kona Coast is all about (never mind these rumors about marijuana crops and bizarre real estate scams).

Kicking ass in Kona means rumbling into the harbor and up to the scales at sunset with a *Big* Fish, not three or four small ones, and the crowd on the pier understands this. They will laugh out loud at anything that can be lifted out of a boat by anything less than a crane.

There is a definite blood-lust in the air around the scales at sundown. By five the crowd is drunk and ugly. People on their first vacation out of Pittsburgh are standing around on the pier and talking like jaded experts about fish the size of the compact cars they just rented out at the airport.

"How big is that thing, Henry?"

"It's *real* big, dear. The sign on the scale says one-twenty-two, but that's probably just the head. The body looks about the size of a cow; I'd guess about a thousand."

The action around the scales on the pier in Kailua Bay at sundown is serious drama, and the tension picks up as each new boat comes in. By five o'clock on a good day they are yelling for thousand-pounders, and woe to the local charter captain who shows up with anything small.

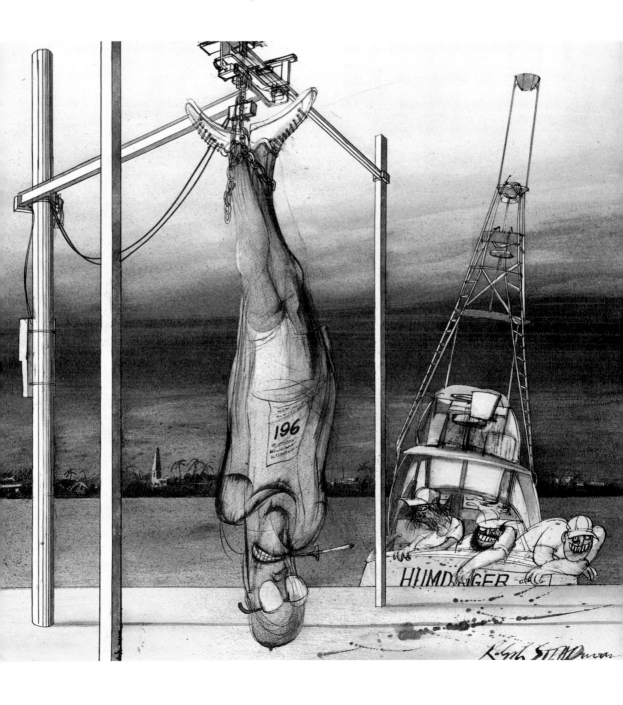

But there is no escape from the judgment of the crowd, because even a 100-pound ahi can be sold off to the icehouse Japs for $2.78 a pound in June—enough to pay off the whole day's fuel and cruising costs—and the price of not bringing it into the scales for the crowd to see and the Japs to buy is too high for any serious skipper to pay. They charge a lot of money for services rendered, and one of these services is getting their clients photographed on the pier with any fish they caught— even a fine little 90-pound marlin that might have almost torn the arms off the person who caught it and that everybody on the boat has been telling him—right up to that moment of truth on the scales—"must be at least five hundred."

All fish look huge when they jump 20 feet straight up in the air on the end of your line and 200 yards aft of the boat. And a hundred pounds feels like a million, after you've fought it for two or three hours; and, for $500 a day, most clients have already fallen in love with the thing anyway, by the time they reel it in.

They want that 8 × 10 color photograph that comes with bringing it into the pier and having it hoisted up on the gallows in full view of the whole crowd, for good or ill. The only thing worse than coming in with a "rat" is coming in with nothing at all.

James King was equally troubled. He had been the first of the shore party to learn of the theft of the cutter. He had been hailed by Burney as he was rowed close by the *Discovery* en route to the *Resolution*. Clerke had just returned to his ship, and King arrived on board at the critical moment when Cook had decided on the more positive and dangerous action.

When King began to recount the details of the previous evening's occurrences, Cook had interrupted him "with some eagerness," as King reported. "It is my intention, Mr. King," Cook had announced grimly, "to bring on board and detain the king and some of the chiefs as hostages against the return of the cutter." Cook completed to his satisfaction the loading of his musket. "Your business is to quiet the minds of the indians on your side of the bay. Inform them that they will not be hurt. And, Mr. King, keep your party together and on their guard."

King stepped into his boat just before his captain embarked in the pinnace. He watched the pinnace, escorted by Williamson in the launch and Lanyon in the small cutter, proceed north from the *Resolution* towards the landing place at Kaawaloa. King landed on the beach by the *heiau* and was met by Bayly, who was anxiously awaiting news. The hostile murmur was scarcely audible here, being carried away on the easterly wind. But there was an atmosphere of tense expectation among the marines, carpenters, sailmakers and others in the encampment, as well as among the natives who stood about uneasily.

Several canoes had been launched, including one under the command of that important and vigorous Chief Kalimu, but had been deterred from paddling far out into the bay by the fate of the canoe from Kaawaloa. King remembered Cook's last words, ordered Ledyard to post his men with muskets loaded with ball, and to open fire under provocation, and then proceeded to High Priest Koa's house.

Koa and his priests were in a nervous condition. "I explained to them, as well as I could, the object of the hostile preparations," King wrote in his report. "I found that they had already heard of the cutter's being stolen, and I assured them that though Captain Cook was resolved to recover it, and to punish the authors of the theft, yet that they and the people of the village on our side need not be under the smallest apprehension of suffering any evil from us."

Richard Hough

The Last Voyage of Captain James Cook

FUCK YOU, I'M RICH

Ralph's tragic and unexpected departure from the islands had left me with a swarm of odd problems, some of them far more serious than the fate of Sadie's dog. Half of Ackerman's marijuana crop had been ripped off sometime during the night when he was on the boat with us at South Point, by cops or somebody else. Either way, he said, it was time to harvest the rest of it and get out of town for a while. "They'll be back, for sure," he said, "and if it was the cops they'll have a warrant next time. I have to yank it *now*. We're talking about two hundred thousand dollars."

There was also the problem of Mr. Heem, the realtor, who wanted the rent for the compound—at least two thousand in cash, and questions would certainly be raised about the crust of red scum on the property. Once it hardened, only an industrial sandblaster could get it off.

I liked the color, myself. It brought back oriental memories. There was a strange red glow on the whole property in the afternoon hours. I drove past it a few times and noticed that even the grass on the lawn seemed to glitter. The swimming pool appeared to be full of blood, on some days, and the dense green foliage on the lemon trees seemed about to burst into flame. The place had a different look now, an air of mystery and magic. Strange and powerful things had happened here. And perhaps they would happen again. There was a certain beauty to it, but the effect was very unsettling and I could see where Heem might have trouble renting it to decent people.

"Pay him off and don't argue," Ackerman advised. "Two thousand is cheap to get rid of swine like Heem. He can cause you a lot of trouble. A lawsuit could drag on for years."

Heem was a powerful figure in local politics. He had once been the president of the Kona Real Estate Board, but a scandal caused him to quit. "He was selling nonexistent condos to pension funds," Ackerman explained. "Xeroxing deeds in triplicate, stealing from old people. Jesus, half the dead construction projects on this island are Heem's work. He's so crooked that he has to screw his pants on every morning, but he's rich and he keeps gangs of lawyers on retainer to put people like you in Hilo Prison."

I agreed that it would be a far far better thing to pay Mr. Heem off at once, but I didn't have the money. I had given him two thousand up front, and the rest of the debt was Ralph's.

"Good luck," said Ackerman. "We're both in trouble now. Our

only hope is the crop. All I have to do is put it in garbage bags and get it to the airport."

"Why not?" I said.

It made no sense at all, but my mood was getting loose and my fiancée had gone off to China for a few weeks, leaving me alone in a weird situation. I relaxed on Ackerman's deck with a thermos of margaritas while he supervised the last few hours of the harvest, and came up with a foolproof plan. He was talking about a lot more than two hundred thousand dollars. It was more like a million. We would bag the whole crop and mail it to a post office box in rural Texas, where a man who'd once cheated me maintained an abandoned ranch. A load like that, I figured, would attract either a massive amount of attention or none at all, and I could live with it either way. If we got there in two weeks and found people hanging from telephone poles, we would know not to go to the post office. But if the coast was clear, we'd be rich. I knew people in Houston who would pay a hundred thousand just for the rights to pick it up. There are people who wait all their lives for one chance to do something like that:

"Howdy. I'm DeLorean, new foreman at the Triple Six. Any mail for me?"

The next few seconds are the ones people pay for, a high wild rush in the nerve ends and your whole life hanging. Whatever happens next will be serious. There is nothing in Vegas or even drugs that comes close to *that* kind of high, they say. There are only two ways to leave a post office in east Texas, once you've signed for a hundred Primo beer crates filled with Hawaiian marijuana. Some people get ambushed by G-men, hauled off in chains or gunned down in a public shootout, and others buy stamps or read the WANTED posters while the hired hands load up the truck, under the watchful eyes of the postmaster.

Ackerman said the risk seemed acceptable to him, so we drove down the mountain to the King Kam Hotel and checked in. Ralph had made all the proper arrangements for the care of his dog, but he hadn't mentioned keepers and the desk clerk was nervous when I said we'd be moving into Mr. Steadman's suite for the duration of the crisis. I had already spoken to the hotel doctor, who said he'd been drinking when he signed a statement of Medical Responsibility for the animal and now regretted it. "This is not your normal *poi* dog," he told me. "It's a monster chow of some kind. When I weighed it today it was five pounds heavier than it was yesterday. The body is growing like a mushroom but the whole central nervous system is gone."

"Don't worry," I said. "I raised the beast from a puppy. It was my Christmas present to Mr. Steadman's daughter."

"Ye gods," he muttered. "What did she give you?"

"Nothing half as valuable as Rupert," I said. "This dog will sire a whole line when we get him to England."

"That's a horrible thought," said the doctor. "If I had a dog like this, I'd have it put to sleep."

"The decision is out of our hands," I said. "Mr. Steadman has left his instructions. Our job is to carry them out."

The doctor agreed. And so did the desk clerk, but some of the details eluded him. "Somebody's going to have to sign for this," he said, "and it can't be the dog." He looked down at the bill in his hands. "Who is 'Rupert'?" he asked. "That's the only billing signature I can authorize."

Who indeed? I thought. I stared intently at the bridge of his nose. Rupert was the dog's name, but I knew the clerk wouldn't stand for it. Ackerman was out in the parking lot with ten garbage bags of raw marijuana, ready to load it onto the elevator and up to Ralph's room on a dolly. There was no going back now. "Don't worry," I said. "Mr. Rupert will be here soon. He'll sign whatever you want."

Just then Ackerman appeared in the lobby, gesturing angrily as he came toward the desk. "Ah ha," I said, "Mr. Rupert." He looked puzzled.

"You'll have to sign," I said. "The dog is too sick."

"Of course," he replied, "I have the cure for the poor beast right here." He reached into his shopping bag and brought out a handful of red and yellow flea collars—Alii colors. The clerk's voice took a different tone.

"Ah yes . . . the dog. I remember now. Of course. Dr. Ho was very concerned. The animal in 505." He checked the computer. "And also 506," he said quickly, with a hint of bad nerves in his voice.

"What?" I said.

"That animal should be put to sleep!" the clerk yelled suddenly. "He's covered with *millions* of red fleas! We can't even *go in* those rooms, much less rent them out! That stinking animal is costing us three hundred dollars a day!"

"I know," said Ackerman. "I have to *live* with the poor brute. Mr. Steadman made me *swear*, just before he went back to London. He wants that dog on a plane just as soon as it's fit to travel."

"Rupert is *our* responsibility now," I said to the clerk. "*All* of us."

"Rupert?" said the clerk.

"Never mind," Ackerman snapped. "Dr. Ho has arranged for special care. Don't worry about the cost. Money means nothing to Mr. Steadman."

"That's right," I said. "He's the richest artist in England."

The clerk nodded respectfully. . . .

"And we're the ones who made him that way. . . ." I pulled Ackerman up to the counter.

"This is Mr. Rupert," I said. "Mr. Steadman's personal manager. He'll handle any red tape."

Ackerman smiled warmly and extended his hand, which was still a faded blue color. The clerk hesitated, clearly disturbed by the corpse-like coloration of Mr. Rupert's flesh . . . but there was blond hair on the arm, and it was wearing a gold Rolex. The clerk's eyes were wary but I saw his nerves relaxing. We were clearly people of substance, despite fits of eccentric behavior.

"My pleasure, Mr. Rupert," he said, reaching out to shake Ackerman's hand. "We'll help you in every way."

"Thank you," said Ackerman. "We'll have a real tragedy on our hands if this animal can't be cured."

"Don't worry," said the clerk. "Dr. Ho is highly respected. That's why we chose him to be the hotel physician."

"Indeed," I said. "He's still treating my infection from the wasp stings."

The clerk nodded blankly, then reached under the counter for an American Express form, which he proferred discreetly to Ackerman. "Now if you'll just sign this," he said.

Ackerman scrawled quickly on the form and accepted two keys from the clerk.

"505 was Mr. Steadman's room," the man said. "But we've opened the connecting doors to 506—so now you have the whole Queen Kalama suite, with a wet bar and all the room you need for that filthy dog."

We thanked him and walked away toward the elevators, but he called after us: "You understand, of course, that the entire Queen Kalama suite is off limits to hotel personnel."

Ackerman stopped in mid-stride, then turned slowly around on his heels like a robot, not smiling this time.

"What do you mean—off limits?"

The clerk was shuffling again. "Well . . . ah . . . I think it's a medical problem, Mr. Rupert. Red fleas are a health hazard. We can't have our employees exposed to infectious disease." He was getting excited again. "Those goddamn things carry germs!" he shouted. "Red fleas are worse than rats! They carry smallpox! They carry cholera! They carry syphilis!"

"What about our room service?" I asked.

The clerk hesitated. His eyes were not focused. "Room service?" he echoed. "Ah yes . . . well . . . ah . . . don't worry about room service. That's no problem at all, Mr. Rupert. You'll have all the room service you need—we'll just have to leave everything outside the door." He nodded happily, clearly pleased with his own quick thinking. "That's right," he went on, "the *rooms* are off limits; but the hallway, of course, is not—so I'll simply advise our room service people never to enter your rooms, for any reason. They can bring anything you want to your doorway, but not across the threshold—is that all right?"

Ackerman nodded thoughtfully, as if pondering grave medical implications. . . . Then he smiled at the clerk and said, "Of course. That's our only solution, isn't it? We'll do business at the door—no risk, no responsibility."

They led Cook and Phillips straight to Terreeoboo's house, a thatched hut built without ostentation or decoration and little larger than its neighbours. The two officers waited outside for the king to appear, and when he failed to do so after some minutes, Cook said, "Would you please investigate, Mr. Phillips. It would not be suitable for me to do so, and I doubt the old gentleman's being inside."

Phillips ducked into the house. "I found the old gentleman just awoke from sleep," said Phillips later. He then told the king that Cook was outside and wished to see him. Slowly, hesitantly, because of his age and condition, the king arose and put on a cloak. Phillips helped him outside, where Terreeoboo showed every sign of pleasure at seeing god Lono, and betrayed no evidence of guilt. . . .

[Cook] turned to Phillips and said in English, "He is quite innocent of what has happened, of that I am convinced." Then he asked the king in Polynesian if he would come on board the *Resolution* with him. King Terreeoboo at once agreed and got to his feet again, with the aid of a son at each elbow, and the party began the walk to the shore. . . .

Events now moved forward at an accelerating rate towards a disaster for which only Cook himself appeared unprepared. His first reaction to the detention of the king was one of anger—a fierce outburst which neither the king nor his wife had ever witnessed before. The king himself had in fact suddenly become a pathetic and un-regal figure—"dejected and frightened" were the words Phillips used.

At the same time the news of the death of Chief Kalimu off Waipunaula arrived with the four canoeists who had witnessed the shooting, and spread with the speed of sound through this emotionally charged gathering. They closed in, two or three thousand already, the sound that had once been like a distant murmur now rapidly growing in volume and undisguised hostility, and with a new sharpness now added to it—the mournful shriek of conch-shells being blown. Even Cook could no longer disregard the great press of numbers about them, and their menacing mood. Not one of them even the nearest, was now prostrated. On the contrary, they were waving clubs and spears, and some of them held high the newly-acquired and prized *pahoas* from the ships' forges, some with blades as long as 20 inches.

Richard Hough

The Last Voyage of Captain James Cook

It sounded very precise, and the clerk nodded eagerly.

So did I, as we moved once again toward the elevators. "A basic canon of all English-speaking jurisprudence," I muttered. "*Nobody* would argue with that logic!"

"Right," said Ackerman. "Oxford Law, one of the first things they taught us."

"Very clean," I replied. "Very legal—Mr. Steadman would want it that way."

Ackerman shrugged. "We'll see," he said quietly. "We could run up a hell of a bill before this thing is over—maybe five hundred dollars a day with room service and doctors. Hell, I just laid out forty-eight dollars in cash for these flea collars. We should have put them on Steadman's plastic."

"How many did you get?" I asked as we stepped into the elevator.

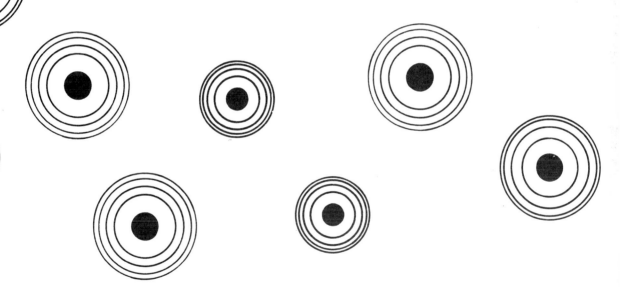

"Two dozen," he said. "Twelve for you and twelve for me. We can wear six on each arm, like bracelets."

"That's good thinking," I said.

The elevator door opened and we stepped inside.

"What name did you sign?" I asked him.

"Rupert," he said.

"That's all?"

"Yeah, but I put a lot of long swirls in it, plenty of old English filigree." He shrugged. "What the hell? It's a dog's signature anyway. My name's not Rupert."

"It is now," I said. "You *are* Mr. Rupert and the first time

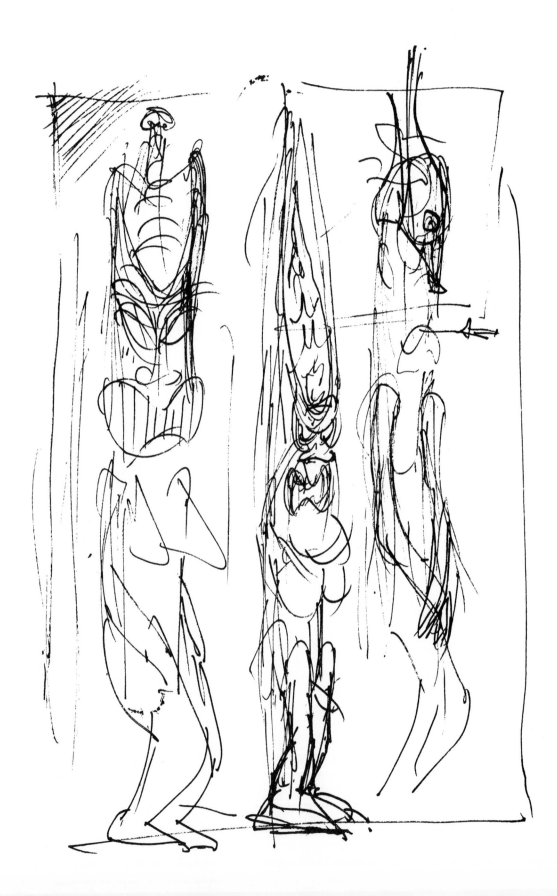

you forget it we'll be in Hilo Prison for defrauding an innkeeper. That's a felony."

He nodded, turning the key in the lock of 506. "Okay," he said finally. "You're right. That dog just got a new name—what is it?"

"Homer," I said. "The dog's name is Homer. I'll have Dr. Ho put it on some kind of affidavit."

"That's right," he said. "Those bastards down at the desk don't care what our names are, anyway. They'll give us whatever we want if Ralph's plastic checks out."

"Jesus," he added. "Is Ralph the kind of guy who pays his bills on time?"

"Probably not," I said. "How much time do we need?"

"Not much," he replied. "I can bag the whole crop in three days—and I like that 'off limits' gig; we won't have to worry about the maids coming in."

I nodded. This was a whole different side of the coin and it worried me. We could deal, I felt, with the Dog Problem—or even the risk of signing a young chow's name on Ralph's credit card, but I was not entirely at ease with Ackerman's plan to use the best suite in the King Kamehameha Hotel, in the heart of downtown Kona, as a bag-house for his whole marijuana crop. He wanted to hire a garbage compactor and crush a whole orchard of marijuana trees into fifty-pound cubes about the size of a TV set.

"How much do you have?" I asked him.

"Not much," he said. "Maybe five hundred pounds."

"What?" I said. "Five hundred pounds! That's too much. They'll smell it. We'll be busted."

"Don't worry," he said. "The whole suite is off limits. They can't cross the threshold."

"Balls," I said. "They can cross anything they want for five hundred pounds. The last thing we need right now is a parade of dope dealers in and out of this place. The whole town would come down on us. It would be a civic outrage; red fleas are one thing, but . . ."

"Never mind," he said. "I *need* the fleas. We couldn't ask for a better cover."

I thought for a moment, then put my worries aside. This was, after all, Mr. Rupert's suite, not mine—and it was Mr. Rupert who would be signing all the room service chits. I was only here as a personal favor to my old friend Steadman, the rich and famous British artist. He had flown back to London on short notice and left us to care for his dying dog. The beast was too sick to touch. Its brain had shorted out a long time ago from the constant plague of red fleas that it had obviously picked up in Hawaii—perhaps in this very hotel. We had no choice,

PROPERTY DEVELOPMENT COMES TO HAWAII.

as I saw it, and I knew Dr. Ho would agree.

"Don't worry about that crazy little quack," Ackerman assured me. "He's the worst coke whore on the island. I've known him for years. He works for me."

"What? Dr. Ho?"

"Yeah. He has friends in Waikiki. They ship a lot of dog medicine." He smiled. "And they ship it in real big crates."

Big crates? I thought. Dog medicine? Indeed. Ralph would want it this way.

By the end of the second week at the hotel, it was clear that we needed a break. The tension was running high. We had been there too long and the locals were getting nervous. The real estate bund had been worried from the start about the harmful effects our story might cause in their market, and our horrible experience in the Jackpot Tournament had done nothing to ease their fears.

And neither had we, for that matter. My own mood, in the aftermath of the fishing tournament, was too foul to hide. Captain Steve was drinking heavily, Norwood had gone into hiding, the beach thugs were still chasing Laila, and Ralph's sudden departure for London—leaving, as he did, in a highly visible wake of shame, failure and public humiliation—was a sure sign to even our friends that whatever we finally published would not be good for business.

Which was, after all, the whole point. That had been understood from the start—although not properly, by some people—and the business of Kona *is* business. Specifically, the selling of real estate. There are 600 registered realtors in the Kona Coast alone, and the last thing they need right now is an outburst of bad publicity in the mainland press. The market is already so overpriced and overextended that a lot of people are going to have to go back to fishing for a living, if things don't change pretty soon. The bull market of the early Seventies is just another Hawaiian legend now, like the hubris of Captain Cook.

DRIVING THE SADDLE ROAD

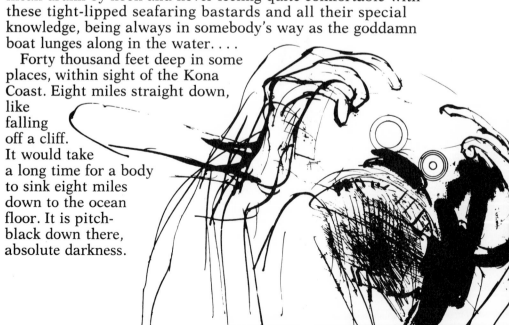

When Ackerman got back from Honolulu we decided to lie low for a while. Even our fishermen friends at Huggo's were getting nervous about why I was still hanging around, three weeks after Ralph left. The rumors filtering down—or up, as it were—from the real estate bund were beginning to take root all around us. I knew we had reached a breakpoint when even the bartenders at the Kona Inn began saying "I thought you left last week" every time I came in; or, "What kind of story are you *really* writing?"

"Never mind," I'd say, "we'll know soon enough." It was my habit, at the time, to hunker down in the afternoon at the far end of the Kona Inn bar to read the newspapers and drink cold margaritas while I kept an eye on the scales across the bay— just in case I saw signs of a crowd gathering, which was usually the sign of a big one coming in.

From my perch at the end of the bar, with the big wooden fans whirling slowly above my head, I could look out on the whole waterfront. It was a good place to relax and read the papers—with the hula class practicing on the lawn, tall coconut palms along the seawall, big sailboats out in the bay and a whole zoo of human weirdness churning quietly all around me.

We were drifting into a macho way of life. There was no doubt about it. And no help for it, either. We were living with these people, dealing with them twenty-four hours a day on their own turf—which was usually out at sea, on their boats, mean-drunk by noon and never feeling quite comfortable with these tight-lipped seafaring bastards and all their special knowledge, being always in somebody's way as the goddamn boat lunges along in the water. . . .

Forty thousand feet deep in some places, within sight of the Kona Coast. Eight miles straight down, like falling off a cliff. It would take a long time for a body to sink eight miles down to the ocean floor. It is pitch-black down there, absolute darkness.

Not even sharks swim that deep. But they will probably get you on the way down, somewhere in that hazy blue level around 300 feet, where the light begins to fade. Bobbing around on a boat the size of a pickup truck in 40,000 feet of blue water is not a good place to get weird with anybody, much less the captain of the boat. Or even a deckhand. Nobody at all.

These are the rules. You do what they say, no matter how crazy it seems even if the captain locks himself in the head below decks at nine o'clock in the morning with a quart of Wild Turkey while the boat runs in circles for forty-five minutes and the deckhand has passed out in the fighting chair with his eyes rolled back in his head like white marbles.

Even then, it is risky to question anything. These people are professional fishermen, skippers, licensed captains, and they take themselves very seriously. Words like "macho" and "fascist" take on a whole new meaning when you lose sight of land. Nothing will turn a man into a nazi any faster than taking a bunch of ignorant strangers out to sea on his boat, regardless of how much they pay. It is almost a rule of the sea, with these charter captains, that "the clients" will panic and do everything wrong at the first sign of trouble, so that is the way they play it; marine insurance is hard to get once you've lost a few clients overboard in water eight miles deep.

"Not one of you swine could get a job in the Caribbean," I said one night to a table full of professional fishermen on the whiskey deck at Huggo's. "You couldn't even get work in Florida."

Their reaction was sullen. The mood of the table went sour, and Ackerman called for the check. It was something like $55, which he paid with his Merrill-Lynch credit card while the others wandered off to look for fights.

"It's time to leave," I told him as we pulled out of the parking lot. "I'm losing my sense of humor."

"So are they," he replied.

The traffic was bumper-to-bumper on Alii Drive, jammed up by a crowd of thugs who had swarmed onto the road to stomp the driver of a motorcycle that had gone out of control and plowed into a gang of surfers. There were forty or fifty of them, all crazy on marijuana.

I made a quick U-turn and aimed for the hotel, avoiding the madness outside. Moments later, from the balcony, we heard the familiar howl of police sirens.

Ackerman opened a new bottle of scotch and we sat down to watch the sunset. It was low tide, with no surf, and the melee out on the highway had cleared the rabble off the beach. It was time, I felt, to relax and ponder the sea.

Ackerman was smoking heavily. His face had taken on a sort of glazed appearance that made conversation awkward.

"Well," he said finally, "let's go to the volcano. They'll never look for us up there." He laughed and suddenly stood up. "That's it," he said. "We'll make a run for the high ground, maybe run the Saddle Road."

"The Saddle Road?"

"Yeah," he said. "You'll like it. We can go for the record— one hour and seventeen minutes from Hilo to Waimea."

"How far?" I said.

"Fifty-three miles, at top speed."

When in doubt, bore it out.

—Harley Davidson

We were coming into Hilo very fast, running downhill in the rain through a residential district at just under a hundred miles an hour. The speedometer went up to 180, but I was not in the mood for unnecessary risks at this point, so I hit the accelerator and shifted down into second gear. . . . Ackerman screamed something at me as a tin mailbox suddenly appeared right in front of us, but I missed it and punched the gas again as we hit the inside of the curve on a straight bounce and kept going. I had never driven a Ferrari before and it had taken me a while to get the hang of it . . . but now that I finally felt comfortable with the machine, I wanted to push it a bit, lean back and let it run. (Any car that costs $60,000, I felt, was built for some special purpose—and until now I had not understood just exactly what this one had been built for, what it really wanted to do.)

The numbers on the speedometer had fooled me, for a while, into thinking that the Ferrari 308 was made to go fast. But I was wrong about that. A lot of cars will go fast, and I have driven most of them. . . . But I have never driven anything that I would dare to put through a five-mile stretch of downhill S-turns at 100 miles an hour in the rain on a two-lane blacktop highway from 10,000 feet above sea level down to zero in less than ten minutes.

The drop is so steep and so fast that every once in a while, at 100 miles an hour, you get an eerie sense of freefall. It is almost like flying, or falling off a cliff. All the outside noise fades away and your eyes feel big in your head and the focus gets very, very sharp.

We had already broken the record—or at least I *thought* we

had—but I couldn't be sure and Ackerman had gone rigid in the passenger seat, no longer keeping track of the stopwatch. He had been yelling numbers at me every ten or fifteen seconds for almost an hour, but now he was getting nervous. His eyes were wild and his hands were braced on the black leather dashboard. I could see that his confidence was slipping. What he wanted now was a handle, but that was out of the question. We had left all our handles at the top of the hill, in the shadow of Hilo Prison, two minutes ahead of the record and miraculously still alive.

Concentrate, I thought. Stay on the fall line, don't touch the brakes, use the gears and don't blink. . . . This is dangerous, we are almost out of control.

But not quite, and the car had amazing balance. It was finally on its own turf, functioning at the top of its form, and I didn't have the heart to slow it down. Far out in front of us I could see, through the clouds, a white line of surf hitting up on the rocks around Hilo harbor. It stretched off in both directions like a line drawn with chalk, the lush green coast of Hawaii on one side and the deep gray swell of the Pacific on the other. The bay was full of whitecaps, and no boats were out . . . a bleak Sunday morning in Hilo, the capital city of the Big Island. The population is mainly Japanese, who tend to sleep in on Sundays, and not many of whom are good Catholics.

I had already taken this into account, along with other ethnic factors, when the Speed Run was still in the planning stage. . . . About six hours ago, in fact, when the bars closed in Kona and Ackerman let slip that he was planning to leave for a Tuna Tournament in Bimini the next day, or at least very soon . . . which alarmed me, because I had very definite plans to use his new yellow Ferrari to set a new land-speed record for running the Saddle Road.

June 4, 1981
Kona

Dear Ralph,

I am hunkered down in my place at Thug Central, watching the sea puppies out there on the break and running up huge bills while I postpone my departure one day at a time and hang out like some

kind of funky Chinook drunkard up here on the balcony waiting
for the big one to strike, like I always knew it would. . . .

And I can almost *smell* the bastard now, circling out there, just
a few feet away from the hook . . . but this time he's acting different;
this time I think he's interested.

Things have changed since you left, Ralph. I shaved my head
again, for one thing. And I also dropped out of sight . . . but not
out of mind, at least not for Captain Steve. I call him constantly,
about any problem or even any random idea that happens into my
mind: Hunting wild pigs? Typewriter ribbons? Deep Diving on
acid? Why is the Tanaguchi market out of Dunhills? Who rents
jeeps? How far to the volcano? Where is Pele? How fast can a
white man drive on the Saddle Road at sunset? Why am I here?
Who has Da Kine? Where are the fish? Has Rupert called? Can
you cash another check for two hundred? Why won't Norwood
return my calls about sacking the gravesites? Who was Spaulding's
mother? Why can't you get a job?

Usually it is Laila who calls him to ask these questions. Which
makes him doubly nervous, because in his heart he knows it's weird.
But he always returns her calls. And then she calls him back, for
more details . . . so they spend a lot of time together, doing business
and telling jokes.

And getting things done. Which frees my brain a bit and gives
me time to focus. I type all night and prowl the roads by day,
looking for Pele. She hitchhikes a lot, they say, usually in the form
of an old woman. So I do a lot of driving and I pick up many
hitchhikers, especially old women . . . but age is a hard thing to be
sure of at 55 miles an hour; and the lazy shameful truth is that
on any hot afternoon I can be found cruising Alii Drive in my T-top
Mustang picking up women of all ages.

And I grill them, while we drive. Some of them can't handle it:
they weep, they lie, they sing along with the radio and show me
their tits, and a lot of them swear they're in love with me by the
time we get to the Kona Surf parking lot.

That's where I take them, no matter what they say or where they
want to go. I take them all the way out to the end of Alii Drive
and down the hill to that spooky little bay, and all the while I keep
offering them a drink of hot gin out of a pint bottle with no top
on it that I keep on the seat between my legs.

Most of them say they'll do just about anything, just as long
as it's not drinking gin with a 200-pound bald psycho in an open
car at high noon on Alii Drive or in the Kona Surf parking lot.
Which is where I always dump them. Except for the ones who drink
gin . . .

OK
HST

A DOG TOOK MY PLACE

June 10, 1981
Kona

Dear Ralph,

Okay . . . Things are <u>really</u> different now. It took a bit longer than I figured, but I think the Kona nut is finally cracked. About six hours after I finished the last draft on driving the Saddle Road, I was sitting in the fighting chair on a boat called the <u>Humdinger</u> and locked into a desperate struggle with a huge fish—and 17 minutes later I had it reeled up so close to the boat that I was able to reach out and shatter its brain with one crazed swooping blow from the Great Samoan war club.

Nobody patronizes me anymore, Ralph. I can drink with the fishermen now. The big boys. We gather at Huggo's around sundown, to trade lies and drink <u>slammers</u> and sing wild songs about Scurvey. I am one of them now. On the night we caught the big fish I was "cut off" at Huggo's, and last night I was 86'd from the Kona Inn for kicking the owner in the nuts, for no good reason at all. The last thing he said—after inviting us for dinner and picking up the tab for $276—was "Why did you do this to me?" Then his eyes rolled back in his head and he sank down with a terrible groan on that black-rock ledge in the entranceway, where he stayed for an hour and a half and said nothing at all to anybody.

That's what I heard today, when I called to find out if he'd received the roses I sent, by way of apology. . . . Yeah, it was that bad. It was the first time in my life that I ever sent a dozen red roses to a man.

The boys at Huggo's went wild when they heard the story. They laughed like loons and slapped me all over my back, and even restored my bar privileges. They don't like Mardian—the man I kicked in the nuts—because one of the first things he did after buying the Kona Inn was to walk into Huggo's, where the fishermen drink, and say he was going to put the place out of business in six months, and anybody who didn't like it could suck on his black belt.

He is very serious about his karate, and he will probably kick my head off my body the next time I go in there to drink. . . . But I like those fine margaritas at sunset, Ralph, and the Kona Inn is the only place in town that will cash my checks for cash.

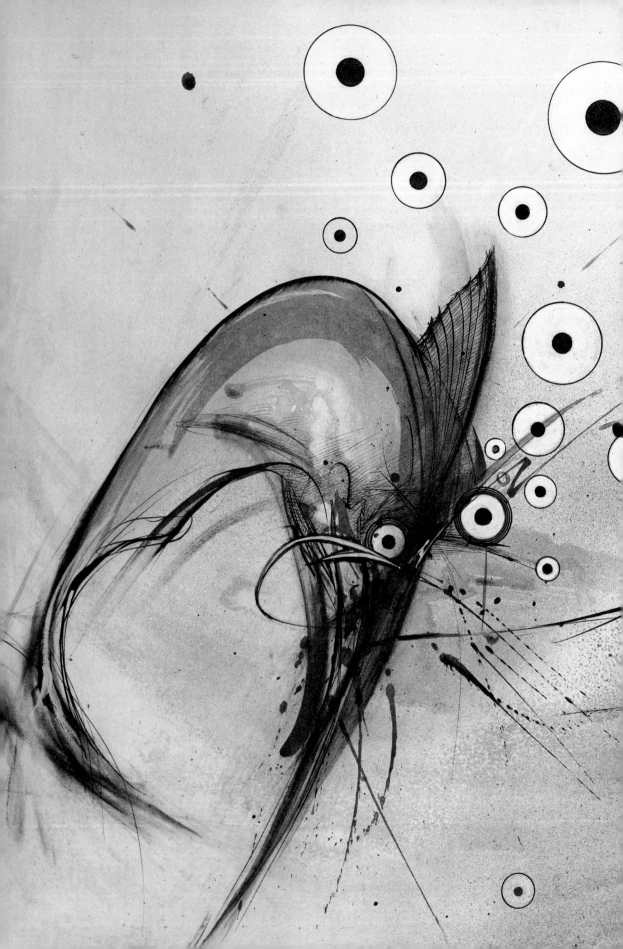

So much for that, eh? I think it's time to leave.

But before I go I want to tell you a fish story. The working title is "How to Catch Big Marlin in Deep Water," but I might want to call it something else by the time we go to press.

This is a weird story, Ralph. It has been weird from the start and it becomes relentlessly weirder with every passing day. They can't understand why I'm still here. And neither can I, for that matter—except that it seemed to be working, despite the brutal expenses.

And they are brutal. Unless this book is a bestseller I will have to get a job out here as either a charter-boat captain or a real estate agent, or maybe even both. That would give me a foothold of sorts—but not for real, and certainly not for long.

I could handle the fishing end, but the real estate market in Kona is so wretched these days that I could own every building on Alii Drive and still go bankrupt by Christmas. The whole coast is for sale to the highest bidder—or to any bidder at all, for that matter. Nobody is buying anything for more than a dime on the dollar. There are 600 real estate agents in Kona, and between them they have made only fifty (50) escrow closures since you left here in early January, six months ago.

That is not what you call a bull market.

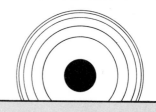

Then one native broke from the crowd following him, advanced with a club, withdrew for fear he might turn, advanced again, raised the club and struck him a fearful blow. Cook staggered for several yards, and fell onto a hand and knee, his musket rattling onto the rocks beside him.

The captain was clearly not killed by this blow, though seriously stunned. Another native did the murder. He was recognized by several onlookers. The muscular Chief Ku'a leapt onto the big stooping form, raised his *pahoa*, and plunged it into the back of Cook's neck. Robust to the end, even this did not kill him. The shock of the blow caused him to fall into a rock crevice full of water from the high tide. Ku'a leapt onto him again, stabbing him repeatedly while others who had joined the murderer attempted to hold him down under the water. In one last gesture of defiance, Cook raised his head. Those in the pinnace saw his big craggy face clearly but momentarily. His lips were forming an unheard cry and he was waving an arm feebly towards them. He attempted to rise, received a second fearful club blow. And now it was all over—all finished except for the dreadful performance of mutilation.

Henry Roberts from Shoreham, Sussex, master's mate, was among those who were unwitting eyewitnesses in the pinnace; and the sight would haunt them all for the remainder of their lives. The natives fell on the corpse like wolves upon a fallen moose, stabbing it, grabbing another's *pahoa* and thrusting it in again, stabbing with spears, too, and hitting it with rocks and clubs. At one point a number of them raised his body from the crevice and beat his head repeatedly against the rock face.

Richard Hough

The Last Voyage of Captain James Cook

But it is <u>our</u> market, Ralph. The chickens are already roosting here, and more come home every day. If we have any real cash by Labor Day we can buy the whole goddamn place, and mete out our own kind of justice.

Right. Yes. And so much for that. It is time to get back to basics. We can always buy real estate, Ralph. And we can always punish the guilty. . . . But right now I think I should tell you the story of what happened when I finally caught a fish.

It was, as you know, my first. And it came at an awkward time. I was ready to leave. We had an eight o'clock flight to Honolulu, then an overnight haul to LA and Colorado. Fuck these people. Their lies are costing us money and I was losing my sense of humor.

That was when I decided to have one last talk with the remnants of Team 200: a business meeting, of sorts; ten o'clock sharp at the Yacht Club—just ask a few critical questions, get the answers on tape, then get out of town the next day.

But the whole idea went wrong, due to booze, and by midnight my mood had turned so ugly that I decided—for some genuinely perverse reason—to go out and fish for marlin once again. It would be my last day in Kona and the plane didn't leave until eight, so why not?

I was still typing in a fit of cold rage when the sun came up and I realized that it was time, once again, to drive down to Union Jack Liquors for another two cases of Heineken, then back in the T-top Mustang for another high-speed run on the highway out there to the Honokahua and another long day at sea.

That will tell you all you need to know about my attitude at that point. I didn't pack that goddamn brutal Samoan war club in my seabag for the purpose of crushing ice. There is a fearful amount of leverage in that bugger, and I knew in my heart that by the end of the day I would find a reason to use it. . . . On something: maybe a fish, or maybe the fighting chair. There is a lot of mahogany to work with on a thirty-six-foot Rybovich.

It was almost ten when I came rocketing into the parking lot at something like sixty in low gear and half out of control in a serious four-wheel drift. I missed that burned-out hulk that once belonged to Lee Marvin by six feet or so, then straightened it out and aimed the front wheels at the big tuna tower of the <u>Humdinger</u>. I could see Steve's blue El Camino parked right on the edge of the cliff above the boat. . . .

They heard me coming, they said later, but there was nowhere to run except up to the front of the boat or into the water. So they ran. But not soon enough. The next sound they heard was my brakes locking up and the awful roar of tires skidding sideways on gravel . . . and then a sharp metallic <u>bang</u> as my front bumper nicked the rear of the El Camino just hard enough to make it leap about three feet straight forward, so quick that it looked like a frog jumping.

The whole thing happened in milliseconds, so fast that it seemed like a dream. No damage, no problem . . . but when I walked out to the edge of the cliff with the first case of beer and looked down on them, nobody spoke. It was like talking to pillars of salt.

"Don't worry," I said, "I have another case in the car."

Still nobody spoke.

Jesus, I thought. These bastards are drunk.

Then I realized that they were not looking at me, but at the front bumper of Steve's El Camino, which was very close to the edge. From where they stood, it looked almost ready to fall straight down

on the boat, which would mean certain death for all three of them—either crushed by the falling car, pinned in the wreckage and drowned as the boat sank, or burned alive in a holocaust of flaming gasoline and exploding diesel tanks that would probably destroy the whole harbor and burn out of control for three days.

These things happen. . . . Yeah, and let's jump this one forward a bit and pick up the story.

We had the fish in the boat by noon. My time was 16 minutes and 55 seconds on the line, and another five seconds to whack it stone dead with the club. The beast fought savagely. It was in the air about half the time I was fighting it. The first leap came about ten seconds after I clipped myself into the chair, a wild burst of white spray and bright green flesh about 300 yards behind the boat, and the second one almost jerked my arms off. These buggers are strong, Ralph, and they have an evil sense of timing that can break a man's spirit. Just about the time your arms go numb they will rest for two or three seconds—and then, in that same split second when your muscles begin to relax, they will take off in some other direction like something shot out of a missile-launcher.

It is not like fishing for trout. What we are talking about here is a beast the size of a donkey that is fighting for its life on its own turf. A ten-pound trout might put up an elegant fight, but a 300-pound marlin with a hook in its throat can rip your arm-bones right out of their sockets, then leap right into the boat and snap your spine like a toothpick. The marlin is a very mean fish, and if it ever develops a taste for human flesh we will all be in trouble. People who fish for blue marlin don't even consider big sharks like the mako and the hammerhead a sporting proposition.

Most sharks won't even put up a fight. You can reel a big hammerhead right up next to the boat in ten or fifteen minutes. No problem.

Until you get to that sixteenth minute. That is when the real fun starts, with a hammerhead. They are harder to kill than most Buicks, and getting one into the boat without killing half the crew is a trick that very few marlin fishermen will ever want to learn.

But that is a different story, Ralph, and right now I'm not in the mood for it. People who fish for big sharks usually do it at night, for their own reasons. Some people want to catch fish, and others want to kill them.

Sharks are not hated and feared in Hawaii like they are in the Caribbean. These Kanakas spend half their time in the water, but you never see anything in the newspapers about "shark attacks." Not even the deep coral divers seem to worry much about sharks, except at night, when they tend to get hungry—and I have never heard a surfer even say the word "shark."

142

*Which could mean nothing at all, as you know. They are not
big on words, and they rarely even talk to each other. But anybody
who spends twelve hours a day thrashing around in the surf like a
bait-fish is either half-shark himself or knows something about
them that we don't.*

*And it occurs to me, now that I think on it, that they don't
even worry me. Which is dumb, because I know the bastards are
down there. I have seen them up close, in the waters off the Keys
. . . and now that I've said this, the taboo is broken and the next
time I go down with a tank anywhere in Hawaii some blood-
hungry rogue mako will probably rip both of my legs off.*

OK
HST

High Priest Koa had been told that he was not to return to the
ship without the body of Cook. Several days passed before he
fulfilled his promise. From accounts provided by the girls, it
appeared that King Terreeoboo and his family and entourage of
chiefs had retired to some caves high up in the clifftops. There,
the captain's corpse had been shared out among the highest
chiefs, the hair to one, the scalp to another, the skull to a third,
the hands to another—and the lion's share, so to speak, being
retained by Terreeoboo. High Priest 'Bretannee' Koa's difficult
task was to extract these prized parts from the chiefs, and ar-
range for their return in one parcel.

It was not until 19 February that Priest Hiapo sent a message
that the body was on shore and awaited collection. Clerke in his
pinnace and King in the cutter put off from the *Resolution*, and
under strong guard approached the shore at Kaawaloa. Beneath
flags of peace, a party of priests and chiefs in solemn and ceremo-
nial state paraded on shore with a massive pile of fruit and hogs
from the king. . . . Priest Hiapo carried in his hands a large parcel
wrapped in plaintain leaves and covered with a mourning cloak
of black and white feathers.

'On opening it,' wrote King, 'we found the captain's hands, the
scalp, the skull, wanting the lower jaw, thigh bones and arm
bones.' The hands had been pierced and salt rammed in to pre-
serve them.

(continues)

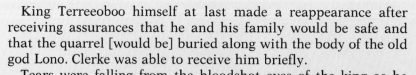

King Terreeoboo himself at last made a reappearance after receiving assurances that he and his family would be safe and that the quarrel [would be] buried along with the body of the old god Lono. Clerke was able to receive him briefly.

Tears were falling from the bloodshot eyes of the king as he begged to know if they would be friends again when they returned to leave behind, as promised, Lieutenant King, the new god Lono. Clerke reassured him, and as he wrote later, 'he expressed great satisfaction and appeared very happy.'

'And when will Lono return?' asked Terreeoboo.

Lieutenant King replied that he would return before long.

Richard Hough

The Last Voyage of Captain James Cook

WE KILLED LIKE CHAMPIONS

June 21, 1981
Kona

Dear Ralph,

Yes . . . the fish was looking <u>me straight in the eye</u> when I
reached far out over the side and bashed his brains loose with the
Samoan war club. He died right at the peak of his last leap: one
minute he was bright green and thrashing around in the air with
that goddamn spear on his nose trying to kill everything within
reach. . . .

And then I smacked him, Ralph. I had no choice. He went limp
with the first hit, about two inches behind the same eye he was
using to look at me . . . and in fact my first instinct was to go for
the eye itself, but I altered my swing at the last split second,
because I knew that kind of hideous mutilation would raise
unpleasant questions at the pier.

Anyway, that should answer your question. After 47 days and
47 nights of dumb shame and futility, that bastard might as well
have been blind in both eyes from birth, for all the mercy he was
going to milk out of me with one final piteous stare. At that point,
I'd have bashed the brains out of a killer whale, if we'd got it up
next to the boat. . . . A terrible blood-lust came on me when I saw
him leaping right beside the boat, so close that he almost leaped
right <u>into it</u>, and when the captain up on the bridge started
screaming "Get the bat! Get the bat! He's gone wild!" I sprang out
of the goddamn fighting chair and, instead of grabbing that silly
little aluminum baseball bat they normally use to finish off these
beasts with ten or fifteen whacks. . . .

That's when I reached into my kitbag and brought out the war
club and kicked Steve out of the way and then, with a terrible shriek,
I hit the beast with a running shot that dropped it back into
the water like a stone and caused about sixty seconds of absolute
silence in the cockpit.

They weren't ready for it. The last time anybody killed a big marlin
in Hawaii with a short-handled Samoan war club was about three
hundred years ago . . . and let me tell you, King Kam was lucky
that fisherman used a paddle on his head, instead of that thing

I swung on the fish; we might never have had any talk about "Laws of the splintered etc. . . ."

Anyway, here's a selection of photos. I wish I could send you more, but it all happened so fast that I had a hell of a time getting any pictures at all . . . I not only had to use the business end of a rod and reel for the first time in my life to drag a 300-pound monster out of the sea in less than twenty minutes and then kill it in the midst of a frenzy right in front of my face, but I also had to rush back into the cabin and get the camera and shoot a whole roll/pack in less than 30 seconds.

Very fast and savage work, Ralph. You'd have been proud of me.

Indeed . . . but the real story of that high-strung blood-spattered day was not so much in the catching of the fish (any fool can do that)—but in our arrival at the pier, which freaked everybody, even Laila.

We came in wild and bellowing, Ralph. They said they could hear me screaming about a half mile out . . . I was shaking the war club at the drunken bastard Norwood on the pier and cursing every booze-crazy incompetent son of a pig-fucking missionary bastard that ever set foot in Hawaii. . . . People cringed and shrunk back in silence, as this terrible drunken screaming came closer and closer to the pier. . . .

They thought I was screaming at them. Nobody on the pier had any idea that I was talking (at the top of my lungs) to Norwood— and the rumbling of our diesel engines was so loud that it seemed to me that I could barely make myself heard.

Which was not the case. They could hear me at the bar in the Kona Inn, 500 yards across the bay . . . and to the big afternoon crowd on the pier, Laila said, it sounded like the second coming of Lono. I raved for fifteen minutes, the whole time it took us to tie up. . . .

The crowd was horrified, and even Laila tried to act like she didn't know us when I hurled a 15-pound ahi at her from about 10 yards out. It hit on the concrete pier with a nasty wet smack, but nobody picked it up, or even spoke . . . they hated everything we stood for, and when I jumped up on the pier and began whipping on the fish with the war club, nobody even smiled.

OK
HST

YESTERDAY'S WEIRDNESS IS TOMORROW'S REASON WHY

June 30, 1981
City of Refuge

Dear Ralph,

Enclosed please find some pages I did in Kona, along with a photograph suitable for framing.

Your letter of 24/6 arrived today, along with the book on shark care, which I suspect we can use. . . . And I also like your notion of the Cro-Magnon man reemerging on the point of a new Ice Age, both ahead <u>and</u> behind his time. Which is a serious trick to pull off, as you know, and it has given me no end of trouble, in both the personal and the professional arenas. Few people are comfortable with this concept, and even fewer can live with it. Thank God I have at least one smart friend like you.

But there is one thing I feel you should know, Ralph, before you take your theory any further: <u>I am Lono.</u>

Yeah. That's me, Ralph. I am the one they've been waiting for all these years. Captain Cook was just another drunken sailor who got lucky in the South Seas.

Or maybe not—and this gets into religion and the realm of the mystic, so I want you to listen carefully; because you alone might understand the full and terrible meaning of it.

A quick look back to the origins of this saga will raise, I'm sure, the same inescapable questions in <u>your</u> mind that it did in mine, for a while. . . .

Think back on it, Ralph—how did this thing happen? What mix of queer and (until now) hopelessly confused reasons brought me to Kona in the first place? What kind of awful power was it that caused me—after years of refusing all (and even the most lucrative) magazine assignments as cheap and unworthy—to suddenly agree to cover the Honolulu Marathon for one of the most obscure magazines in the history of publishing? I could have gone off with a planeload of reporters to roam the world with Alexander Haig, or down to Plains for a talk with Jimmy Carter. There were many things to write, for many people and many dollars—but I spurned them all, until the strange call came from Hawaii.

And then I persuaded <u>you</u>, Ralph—my smartest friend—to not only come with me, but to bring your whole family halfway around the world from London, for no good or rational reason, to spend

what might turn out to be the weirdest month of our lives on a treacherous pile of black lava rocks called the Kona Coast . . .

Strange, eh?

But not really. Not when I look back on it all and finally see the pattern . . . which was not so clearly apparent to me then, as it is now, and that's why I never mentioned these things to you while you were here. We had enough problems, as I recall, without having to come face to face with the Genuinely Weird. Merely getting on and off the island required thousands of dollars and hundreds of man-hours; and the simple act of sending a packet from Kona to Portland, Oregon, was a full-time job for both of us, for three or four days.

And then, when you left, the massive shame and humiliation I suffered at the hands of those fools made me both too crazy to talk about what I was only then beginning to understand was the real reason for it all . . . and in fact I failed to see it clearly, myself, until last night.

Many things happened after you left, Ralph, and that is why I am writing you, now, from what appears to be my new home in The City; so make note of the address:

c/o Kaleokeawe
City of Refuge
Kona Coast, Hawaii

You remember the Kaleokeawe, Ralph—it's the hut where you told me they were keeping King Kam's bones; the place where you dared to climb over the wall and pose in the yard for some Polaroid shots, like the buggering fool you are and always will be. . . .

What?

Did I say that?

Well . . . yeah, I did . . . but never mind these idle jabs, Ralph; you weren't there when the deal went down.

The trouble began on the day I caught the fish—or, more specifically, it began when I came into the harbor on the flying bridge of the _Humdinger_ and started bellowing at the crowd on the dock about "filthy drunken sons of missionaries" and "lying scum" and "doomed pig-fuckers" and all those other things I mentioned in my last update letter.

What I _didn't_ tell you, old sport, is that I was also screaming, "_I am Lono!_" in a thundering voice that could be heard by every Kanaka on the whole waterfront, from the Hilton to the King Kam—and that many of these people were deeply disturbed by the spectacle.

I don't know what got into me, Ralph—I didn't mean to say it—at least not that loud, with all those natives listening. Because they are _superstitious people_, as you know, and they take their legends seriously. Which is understandable, I think, in the minds of people who still shudder at the memory of what happened when they bungled Lono's _last_ visit.

It was not surprising, in retrospect, that my King Kong-style arrival in Kailua Bay on a hot afternoon in the spring of 1981 had a bad effect on the natives. The word traveled swiftly up and down the coast, and by nightfall the downtown streets were crowded with people who had come from as far away as South Point and the Waipio Valley to see for themselves if the rumor was really true—that Lono had, in fact, returned in the form of a huge drunken maniac who dragged fish out of the sea with his bare hands and then beat them to death on the dock with a short-handled Samoan war club.

By noon the next day these rumors of native unrest had reached our friends in the real estate bund, who saw it as the "last straw," they said later, and reached a consensus decision to get me out of town on the next plane. This news was conveyed to me by Bob Mardian at the bar of the Kona Inn, which he owns.

"These guys are not kidding," he warned me. "They want to put you in Hilo Prison." He glanced nervously around the bar to see who was listening, then grasped my arm firmly and leaned his head close to mine. "This is serious," he whispered. "I've got three waitresses who won't come to work until you're gone."

"Gone?" I said. "What do you mean?"

He stared at me for a moment, drumming his fingers on the bar. "Look," he said finally. "You've gone too far this time. It's not funny anymore. You're fucking with their _religion_. The whole town is stirred up. The realtors had a big meeting today, and they tried to blame it on _me_."

I called for another brace of margaritas—which Mardian declined, so I drank them both—while I listened. It was the first time I'd ever seen Mardian take anything seriously.

"This Lono thing is dangerous," he was saying. "It's the one thing they really believe in."

I nodded.

"I wasn't here when it happened," he went on, "but it was the first thing I heard about when I got off the plane—'Lono is back, Lono is back.'" He laughed nervously. "Jesus, we can get away with almost anything out here—but not _that_."

The bar was quiet. People were staring at us. Mardian had obviously been chosen—by his own people—to deliver an ugly message.

OK
HST

(24 hours later) . . . I must be getting old, Ralph, eight pages is about all I can do in one night; so I took a break and got some sleep. I also felt I should back off and have a long look at this I am Lono business, because I was wary of being fooled by another false dawn.

That was the problem, Ralph. We were blind. The story we wanted was right in front of our eyes from the very start—although we can be excused, I think, for our failure to instantly understand a truth beyond reality. It was not an easy thing for me to accept the fact that I was born 1,700 years ago in an ocean-going canoe somewhere off the Kona Coast of Hawaii, a prince of royal Polynesian blood, and lived my first life as King Lono, ruler of all the islands.

According to our missionary/journalist, William Ellis, I "governed Hawaii during what may in its chronology be called the Fabulous Age" . . . until "(I) became offended with my wife, and murdered her; but afterwards lamented the act so much, as to induce a state of mental derangement. In this state (I) traveled through all the islands, boxing and wrestling with everyone (I) met . . . (I) subsequently set sail in a singularly shaped 'magic' canoe for Tahiti, or a foreign country. After (my) departure (I) was deified by (my) countrymen, and annual games of boxing and wrestling were instituted in (my) honor."

How's that for roots?

What?

Don't argue with me, Ralph. You come from a race of eccentric degenerates; I was promoting my own fights all over Hawaii fifteen hundred years before your people even learned to take a bath.

And besides, this is the story. I don't know music, but I have a good ear for the high white sound . . . and when this Lono gig flashed in front of my eyes about 33 hours ago, I knew it for what it was.

Suddenly the whole thing made sense. It was like seeing The Green Light for the first time. I immediately shed all religious and rational constraints, and embraced a New Truth.

It has made my life strange and I was forced to flee the hotel after the realtors hired thugs to finish me off. But they killed a local haole fisherman instead, by mistake. This is true. On the day before I left, thugs beat a local fisherman to death and left him either floating facedown in the harbor, or strangled to death with a brake-cable and left in a jeep on the street in front of the Hotel Manago. News accounts were varied. . . .

154

That's when I got scared and took off for The City. I came down the hill at ninety miles an hour and drove the car as far as I could out on the rocks, then I ran like a bastard for the Kaleokeawe— over the fence like a big kangaroo, kick down the door, then crawl inside and start screaming "I am Lono" at my pursuers, a gang of hired thugs and realtors, turned back by native Park Rangers.

They can't touch me now, Ralph. I am in here with a battery- powered typewriter, two blankets from the King Kam, my miner's headlamp, a kitbag full of speed and other vitals, and my fine Samoan war club. Laila brings me food and whiskey twice a day, and the natives send me women. But they won't come into the hut—for the same reason nobody else will—so I have to sneak out at night and fuck them out there on the black rocks.

I like it here. It's not a bad life. I can't leave, because they're waiting for me out there by the parking lot, but the natives won't let them come any closer. They killed me once, and they're not about to do it again.

Because I am Lono, and as long as I stay in The City those lying swine can't touch me. I want a telephone installed, but Steve won't pay the deposit until Laila gives him $600 more for bad drugs.

Which is no problem, Ralph; no problem at all. I've already had several offers for my life story, and every night around sundown I crawl out and collect all the joints, coins and other strange offerings thrown over the stakefence by natives and others of my own kind.

So don't worry about me, Ralph. I've got mine. But I would naturally appreciate a visit, and perhaps a bit of money for the odd expense here and there.

It's a queer life, for sure, but right now it's all I have. Last night, around midnight, I heard somebody scratching on the thatch and then a female voice whispered, "You knew it would be like this."

"That's right!" I shouted. "I love you!"

There was no reply. Only the sound of this vast and bottomless sea, which talks to me every night, and makes me smile in my sleep.

OK
HST

RAGE, RAGE AGAINST THE COMING OF THE LIGHT

Skinner brought me some whiskey last night. He flew over from Honolulu with two girls from the agency and five or six litres of hot Glenfiddich Scotch, which we drank on the beach in paper cups with some ice I got from the Rangers. The moon was dim and the clouds were low, but we had enough light from my portable hurricane lamp to see each other's faces when we talked. The girls were not comfortable here, and neither was Skinner. "I'm sorry," he said later, "but it's too weird to laugh at."

We were sitting on the floor of my house in the City of Refuge, about thirty miles south of Kailua on the Kona Coast of Hawaii. The girls had gone swimming in the bay, and from where I sat I could see them splashing around in the surf, their naked bodies shining in the moonlight. Occasionally one of them would appear in the small doorway and ask for a cigarette, then laugh nervously and run away again, leaving us alone to our baleful conversation.

The sight of these long-legged nymphs prancing around on the black rocks outside my door made concentration difficult. Skinner could not see the girls from where he sat, and his mood was becoming so grim that I tried not to see them myself. . . . Because I understood that this was not a social visit, and we didn't have much time.

"Look," he was saying. "We're both in trouble."

I nodded.

"And we will both end up in Hilo Prison if we don't put an end to this madness—right?"

That got my attention. "Well . . . ah . . . maybe so," I agreed. "Yeah, you're probably right; it's Hilo Prison for sure. . . ."

My mind flashed back to realities: fraud, arson, bombs, assault, conspiracy, harboring fugitives, heresy . . . all felony charges.

He shook his head and leaned forward to hand me a cigarette. We were both sitting cross-legged on the floor, each on our own tapa mat, with the dull glow of the hurricane lamp like a tiny campfire between us . . . and both our necks bowed with serious problems that could only be solved by serious men thinking serious thoughts.

A noise outside the hut distracted me and I glanced out the door. One of the girls was standing high on the rocks with her hands on her hips and her nipples pointing up at the moon like some ancient Hawaiian goddess curling into a swan dive all the way down to the Land of Po . . . and I was stunned by the sight of it, some elegant vision from a half-remembered past . . . with the sea lapping up on the rocks and the moon rolling over toward China.

"Never mind the girls," Skinner snapped. "We can always take them with us"— he paused, looking up at me—"if we can ever get you out of this place."

He was right. I shifted my position on the floor so I wouldn't have to see the girls, and tried again to focus on what he was telling me. . . .

Sometime around midnight we ran out of ice and I had to use the bullhorn to call for more. Skinner was worried about waking up the natives across the bay, but I assured him they were used to it. "They love the bullhorn," I explained. "Especially the children. Every once in a while I let one of them use it."

"That's dumb," Skinner mumbled. "Stay away from children. They'll betray you by accident. Jesus," he muttered, "a bullhorn! Are you out of your fucking mind? These natives are nervous enough, as it is. If they decide you're a pervert, you're finished."

"But I never turn it on," I said, showing him the ON-OFF-VOLUME switch under a piece of duct tape on the handle. "The little bastards can yell into it all day and it won't make a sound. But when I use it," I said, "it sounds like *this*."

A terrible screech of feedback and distorted low-end rumble filled the *heiau* as I punched the sound level all the way up to 10 watts and aimed it out the door at the Ranger station back in the palm jungle. The sound was unbearable. Skinner leaped to his feet and rushed outside to calm the girls, who were screaming hysterically. . . . But I couldn't hear them now; their voices were completely blotted out. And then, as thunder follows lightning came the strange crackling roar of my own voice—saying very gently and calmly:

"ALOHA!   ICE CUBES, MAHALO."

And then, repeated over and over again, like a voice from the Land of Po, "ICE CUBES, MAHALO, YES, ICE CUBES . . . ICE CUBES . . . MAHALO . . . ICE CUBES . . . ICE CUBES . . . MAHALO."

The relentless screech of the feedback rose and fell like wild electric music along with my words, bellowing across the quiet little bay like the voice of some monster coming out of the sea with a diesel meat-grinder and a brain from another world.

"ICE CUBES! TO THE HEIAU! MAHALO."

I uttered one final wavering burst of oriental gibberish, then tossed the bullhorn aside as Skinner appeared in the doorway, his eyes the size of baseballs. "You crazy bastard!" he screamed, "now we'll never get out of this place!" He grabbed his Hobie seabag off the floor and began frantically jamming things into it.

"Calm down," I said. "The ice is on its way."

He paid no attention. "Fuck ice," he muttered. "I'm leaving."

"What?" I said, still not understanding his frenzy. He was crawling around on the floor like an animal frantic in heat.

Then he stood up and waved a sharp stick at me. "Fuck *off*, dumbo!" he screamed. "It's Hilo Prison for you! You're not even *sane*, man! You want to get us *all* busted!" He shook his stick at me again, as if to ward off a demon. "But not *me*, you bastard! I'm *out* of here! I never want to see these goddamn islands again! Or you either. Jesus," he said. "You're worse than crazy. You're dumb!"

"So what?" I said. "It doesn't matter here."

He stared at me for a moment, then lit a cigarette.

I opened another bottle of Scotch and scraped the rest of the ice out of the cooler. "We'll have more in a minute," I said.

Which was true. The night ranger—probably my friend Mitch Kamahili—was even now on his way along the path through the palm trees with a garbage bag full of ice cubes. In a moment I would see the bright beam of his flashlight sweeping the bay, and I would signal him back with my own light . . . and then I would walk carefully across the rocks to the old canoe beside the main heiau when I knew he would leave the icebag . . . and in its place I would leave my own bag . . . the one from the last night's delivery—full of empty beer bottles, cigarette butts, dead batteries and crumpled wads of blue typewriter paper.

This was our nightly routine, and the rangers seemed to enjoy it. All they asked was that I stay out of sight during the daylight hours when the tourists were roaming around. That would be a flagrant violation of the main kapu.

The gravity of the situation had been explained to me more than once by Mitch, the young ranger who normally worked the graveyard shift. On some nights—when he was sure I had no visitors—he would bring the ice all the way out to the heiau and we would sit for a while, and talk about what was happening.

Or *not* happening, as he'd been very careful to explain to me. "You are *not here*," he told me. "The heiau is kapu. *Nobody* can be here."

I listened carefully, with all three ears, knowing in my heart that he was far crazier than I was.

I was dealing, night after night, with a U.S. National Park Ranger in full uniform who also believed, without question, that any shark he saw in the bay might be his uncle . . . in a different form, perhaps, but still *family*.

On some nights, as we sat there on the edge of the sea drinking beakers of iced malt whiskey and sharing a pipe of the local weed he would suddenly stand up and say, "See you later, boss. I'm going home for a while."

When he got in these moods, Mitch would roll a huge green cigarette and go off to sit by himself. I would see the glow of the cigarette for a while, and then I would hear a splash as he slithered over the side, leaving me to brood drunkenly in the dim glare of the hurricane lamp, hunched on the rocks like a stranded ape.

Over the side. Into the deep, blowing air like a porpoise as he slid away from the rocks and out to the open sea, disappearing into the ocean with the atavistic grace of some mammal finally remembering where it really wanted to be.

The Song of Waahia

O the long knife of the stranger.
Of the stranger from other lands,
Of the stranger with sparkling eyes,
Of the stranger with a white face!
O long knife of Lono, the gift of Lono;
It flashes like fire in the sun;
Its edge is sharper than stone,
Sharper than the hard stone of Hualalai;
The spear touches it and breaks,
The strong warrior sees it and dies!
Where is the long knife of the stranger?
Where is the sacred gift of Lono?
It came to Wailuku and is lost,
It was seen at Lahaina and cannot be found,
He is more than a chief who finds it,
He is a chief of chiefs who possesses it.
Maui cannot spoil his fields,
Hawaii cannot break his nets;
His canoes are safe from Kauai.
The chiefs of Oahu will not oppose him,
The chiefs of Molokai will bend at his feet.
O long knife of the stranger,
O bright knife of Lono!
Who has seen it? Who has found it?
Has it been hidden away in the earth?
Has the great sea swallowed it?
Does the kilo see it among the stars?
Can the kaula find it in the bowels of the black hog?
Will a voice from the anu answer?
Will the priests of Lono speak?
The kilo is silent, the kaula is dumb.
O long knife of the stranger,
O bright knife of Lono,
It is lost, it is lost, it is lost!

The Song of Waahia, A Renowned Prophetess

Waahia lived during the 1200s A.D. Although it is claimed that Waahia was of chieftain lineage, nothing is positively known, even of her parents. Through an almost undeviating verification of her prophecies, in time she became noted and feared by the people, not only as a favored devotee of Uli, the god of the sorcerers, but as a medium through whom the unipihili, or spirits of the dead, communicated. She lived alone in a hut in a retired part of the valley of Waipio, and it is said that a large pueo, or owl, which was sacred and sometimes worshipped, came nightly and perched upon the roof of her lonely habitation.

The Legends and Myths of Hawaii by
His Majesty King Kala-Kaua (1881)